YOUR KNOWLEDGE HAS

- We will publish your bachelor's and
  master's thesis, essays and papers

- Your own eBook and book -
  sold worldwide in all relevant shops

- Earn money with each sale

Upload your text at www.GRIN.com
and publish for free

Tomasz Halapacz

The Theory and Reality of Wireless LAN Security

Final Year project

GRIN Publishing

Bibliographic information published by the German National Library:

The German National Library lists this publication in the National Bibliography; detailed bibliographic data are available on the Internet at http://dnb.dnb.de .

This book is copyright material and must not be copied, reproduced, transferred, distributed, leased, licensed or publicly performed or used in any way except as specifically permitted in writing by the publishers, as allowed under the terms and conditions under which it was purchased or as strictly permitted by applicable copyright law. Any unauthorized distribution or use of this text may be a direct infringement of the author s and publisher s rights and those responsible may be liable in law accordingly.

Imprint:

Copyright © 2011 GRIN Verlag GmbH
Print and binding: Books on Demand GmbH, Norderstedt Germany
ISBN: 978-3-656-92441-8

This book at GRIN:

http://www.grin.com/en/e-book/178977/the-theory-and-reality-of-wireless-lan-security

GRIN - Your knowledge has value

Since its foundation in 1998, GRIN has specialized in publishing academic texts by students, college teachers and other academics as e-book and printed book. The website www.grin.com is an ideal platform for presenting term papers, final papers, scientific essays, dissertations and specialist books.

Visit us on the internet:

http://www.grin.com/

http://www.facebook.com/grincom

http://www.twitter.com/grin_com

Wireless LAN Security

Academic Year 2010-2011

II. ABSTRACT

This paper addresses the theory and reality of Wireless LAN security. It provides an overview of security mechanisms and explains how security works in Wireless LAN networks. An in depth analysis of the Wired Equivalent Privacy (WEP), Wi-Fi protected access (WPA) and WPA2 standards is presented. The security vulnerabilities that exist in them are analysed and explained. In the investigation, a wardriving approach is used. It is observed that about 30% of all WLANs detected during network discovery experiment operate with WEP encryption witch further investigated is proved that can be compromised with 100% success. The author discusses the potential consequences that arise from using a weak encryption. Experimental results of penetrating WPA secured network illustrate how easy it is to protect from dictionary attacks by simply using a combination of strong encryption protocol and complex key. The results of the practical part of the project are used to generate guideline in terms of choosing the right encryption method.

III. CONTENTS

IV. LIST OF FIGURES

V. LIST OF ABBREVIATIONS

ACL   Access Control List

ADSL Asymmetric Digital Subscriber Line

AES   Advanced Encryption Standard

AP   Access Points

BSSID Basic Service Set ID

DHCP Dynamic Host Configuration Protocol

DOS   Denial-of-Service

IEEE Institute of Electrical and Electronics Engineers

IETF Internet Engineering Task Force

IP   Internet Protocol

IPsec Internet Protocol Security

IV   Initialization Vector

LAN   Local Area Network

MAC   Medium Access Control

NIC   Network interface card

PSK   PreShared Key

RC4   Rivest Cipher 4

SSID Service Set IDentifier

SSL   Secure Socket Layer

TK   Temporal Key

TKIP Temporal Key Integrity Protocol

VPN   Virtual Private Network

WEP   Wired Equivalent Privacy

Wi-Fi Wireless Fidelity

WLAN Wireless LAN

WPA   Wi-Fi Protected Access

WPA2 Wi-Fi Protected Access version 2

1. INTRODUCTION

A decade ago hardly anyone heard of wireless internet. Today, however, the IT technology is mostly based on the wireless connection followed by the development of wireless network-enabled devices (Cache and Liu, 2010). The manufacturers of the speed network equipment generate billions of pounds, yet a worldwide usage carries a number of risks costing their business staggering amount of money and resources. In Wireless Local Area Networks (WLAN) major issues are associated with the security problems. The wireless signal of the WLAN is broadcast through the air in all directions simultaneously. An unauthorized user can easily capture this signal using freeware tools to exploit WLAN vulnerability. WLANs are increasingly used within home and business environment due to the convenience, mobility, and affordable prices for wireless devices. WLAN gives mobility and flexibility to users in homes and hot spot environments, such as airports and campuses. The wide range of usage emphasises the importance of having a secure network and protect from potential break ins. In order to do so, mostly encryptions such as WEP and WPA/WPA2 are used (Kizza, 2011). This allows the transmitted data within the network to be encrypted. Nevertheless, the fact that information is said to be encrypted, does not necessarily mean the hacking specialists can access it (Cache and Liu, 2010).

Wireless LAN networks are generally designed with emphasis on convenience rather than security. This is exactly where the problem lies. On a wireless network almost anyone with a WLAN enabled device can easily connect to and penetrate other users systems (Misic, 2008), thus research based and findings will illustrate just how easy it is to protect from malicious attacks by simply using a combination of strong encryption protocol and complex key. The author discusses the potential consequences that arise from using a weak encryption. In order to explore further the findings and results of this study a wardriving test has been conducted to critically assess the issues associated with security and to examine its current level.

This paper looks at the security tools available for WLANs and their practicality in order to increase security awareness. It is demonstrated how to gain unauthorised access to an average wireless network that is using out dated security protocols like WEP. However, the main focus is on the potential risks when using wireless networks and ways to provide an appropriate security.

1.1 AIM AND OBJECTIVES

1.1.1   Aim

To analyse aspects of wireless LAN security and to demonstrate the effects of potential attacks on secured networks

1.1.2   Objectives

- to conduct in depth research of current wireless LAN security and potential issues associated with security
- to establish the operation issues in wireless medium and ways to minimize them
- to discover unsecured wireless access points in Southampton area using "wardrive" technique
- to conduct an experiment of breaking into networks secured by WEP and WPA
- to recommend possible solutions to improve security in WLANs

2. LITERATURE REVIEW

In this chapter, popular WLAN technologies and problems relevant to the research area are introduced. The aim is to provide an overview of wireless LAN securities and to evaluate the WLAN security issues.

2.1.   WIRELESS LOCAL AREA NETWORK

The WLAN developments, maintenance and standard creation is provided by the Institute of Electrical and Electronic Engineers (IEEE), which is the world's leading professional association for the advancement of technology (IEEE, 2011). The IEEE refers to WLAN by its technical name: IEEE 802.11. 802.11 standards cover all versions of WLAN technology. There are different types of 802.11 including B, G, and N, as the most common versions in use today (Burns, 2007). During further developments of 802.11, the IEEE Standards Board specified the types of security available for WLAN communication.

2.1.1 Wireless LAN Security

There are currently three main encryption technologies available to WLAN communication: WEP, WPA, and WPA2. These technologies attempt to provide Confidentiality, Integrity and Authentication (CIA Triad). However, they do not all succeed at these tasks and introduce vulnerabilities into the WLANs.

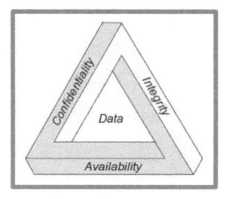

Figure 2-1. CIA Triad (I.S.S.W.G, 2011)

The first protection used in 802.11 networks was Wired Equivalent Privacy (WEP). The author would like to highlight the word "was", as 2 years later WEP encryption algorithm RC4 was broken by Fluhrer, Mantin and Shamir (2001), hence WLAN security gained a bad reputation. In 2003, Wi-Fi Protected Access (WPA) was introduced by the Wi-Fi alliance. It was not the standard but, at the time, it provided a temporary solution to wireless security. Throughout this time, institutions used VPNs as an alternative security solution to secure their wireless networks (Dowt, 2003).

Finally, in 2004, IEEE introduced very strong encryption mode called Counter Mode with Cipher Block Chaining Message Authentication Code Protocol (CCMP) with a new authentication protocol - Advanced Encryption Standard (AES) (IEEE-SA Standards Board, 2004). In result WLAN security developed into a mature and secure solution and its reputation was restored (Kizza, 2011).

2.2.   WEP - WIRED EQUIVALENT PRIVACY

WEP is the original security mechanism of the 802.11b standard (IEEE-SA Standards Board, 2001). As the name (Wired Equivalent) suggests, its intention has never been to make WLAN a 100 per cent secure, but to provide the same security as in a wired network. WEP was built for the encryption of the network traffic, the data integrity and station authentication. These 3 core elements attempt to satisfy the security objectives Authenticity, Integrity and Confidentiality (Howard and Prince, 2010). However, Borisov *et al* (2001) has proved that vulnerabilities exist for each of them; therefore none of the security objectives can be reached. Despite these issues, WEP is still widely deployed, thus it is necessary to explore further its vulnerabilities.

2.2.1 WEP Security Analysis

Leading research of the insecurity of WEP was done by Walker (2000) who concluded that the WEP was unsafe at any key size and that it could not meet its design goal which was to provide data privacy to the level of a wired network. Borisov *et al* (2001) presented the first serious paper on WEP insecurity receiving a high volume of controversy in the press. Only a month later Fluhrer, Mantin and Shamir (FMS) (2001) published a paper called *"Weaknesses in the Key Scheduling Algorithm of RC4"* describing an attack on the 'key scheduling algorithm' used by WEP. The FMS attack was only theoretical, yet it did not take long till it got adapted into the real world. Nevertheless, it was FMS that started the downfall of the WEP. According to Gast (2005) it only took a week for his group of students, including the delivery of the WLAN Card, to crack the WEP key. However, these tests where purely experimental and no easy-to-use tools were available to the public at the time. Yet, this soon changed when an open source tool called AirSnort was released for Linux, allowing anyone with a computer and networking knowledge to hack into a Wireless LAN (AirSnort, 2011).

The first attempt to counter this attack was made by Agere Systems, who developed more secure version of WEP called 'WEPPlus' or WEP+. It greatly reduces the amount of 'weak IV' produced by normal WEP implementations and was released as a firmware update for their own access points (Burns, 2007). Simultaneously, Cisco (2001) decided to go for a different approach and introduced 'Dynamic WEP Keys' to their Aironet WLAN Products. Unfortunately, the issue with solutions discussed above is that they are vendor specific and incompatible with each other.

Matters got worse for WEP in 2004, when a hacker knows as 'Korek' replied to a thread on the Netstumbler forum about WEP security. The attack, he described, was no longer dependent on weak IV. The 'Korek attack' used statistical crypto-analysis and proved to be more efficient than the FMS attack (Beaver and McClure, 2010).

In 2007, a new generation of WEP attacks was published by Tews, Weinmann, and Pyshkin. Their attack called PTW introduced new concepts, which allow breaking into WEP in less than a minute. The KoreK and PTW attacks were quickly integrated into WEP cracking and WLAN auditing tools and are now the standard for attacking WEP protected WLANs (Aircrack-ng, 2010).

2.2.2   How WEP Works

Authentication:

According to Beaver and McClure (2010) process of authentication is used to verify that a valid user is trying to connect to the network. In WEP there are two approaches to do this: open system authentication and shared key authentication.

Open Authentication is not really any authentication at all, because when a station wants to authenticate, the AP always accepts the request and allows a station to join the network.

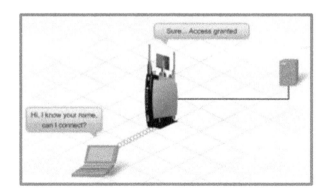

Figure 2-2. Open Authentication (Bel, 2009)

This is a device-based authentication scheme as the user does not need to provide a valid user ID or password. Instead, the MAC address of the connecting node is used to identify it. Borisov (2001) in his early research highlights the possibility to configure the MAC addresses of the permitted clients with their access points. However, this approach does not provide the desired security as it is easy to spoof an address.

Shared key Authentication uses four messages (Figure 2-3). When a station requests Authentication the AP sends a challenge-text in the form of a 40 or 128-bit number. The Station encrypts this text with the WEP secret key, sends it back to the AP which decrypts the text, checks if it is the correct one and then grants access to the network.

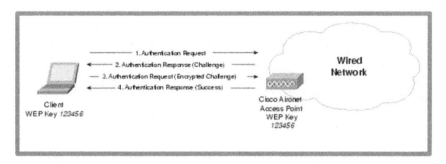

Figure 2-3. WEP authentication process (Cisco Support, 2008)

This process only authenticates the station to the access point, not the other way around; therefore a malicious AP can simply pretend that the authentication was successful without knowing the secret key (Gast, 2005).

Figure 2-4. WEP one way Authentication (Bel, 2009)

WEP uses the RC4 algorithm to encrypt data messages. This algorithm uses a stream cipher meaning that every byte is encrypted individually with the WEP key. The decryption is the reverse of this process and uses the same key (Fluhrer *et al*, 2001). Usually the cipher key has 128 bit and consist of 24 bit initialisation vector (IV and 104 bit key). An IV is used to produce a single key-stream for each frame transmitted. The unique key is sent in plain text with the packet, therefore can be viewed by a packet sniffer (Lockhart, 2006). This is a major flaw of WEP encryption. As said by Flickenger (2006) the fact that the same key is used for all frames transmitted in the WLAN network it makes penetration test much easier.

2.2.3 Conclusion

WEP still provides basic security and it is integrated in most of the routers. A recent survey conducted for the purpose of this project on the Wireless security illustrates that an estimated third of the Access Points have WEP encryption enabled (Chapter 3). Ziarek (2011) confirms these findings with a survey of the security situation in Poland where he found 21 per cent of the WLANs are still WEP encrypted.

2.3.   WPA/WPA2 - WI-FI PROTECTED ACCESS

The design of WPA is based on a Draft 3 of IEEE 802.11i standard. It was proposed to ensure the release of a higher volume of security WLAN products before IEEE group could officially introduce 802.11i. Yet, major weaknesses of the WEP had already been known at the time (IEEE-SA Standards Board, 2004).

Due to those weaknesses, WPA introduced some improvements. First, WPA can either be used with an IEEE 802.1x authentication server, where each user is given different keys or be used in a less secure "pre-shared key" (PSK) mode, where every client is given the same pass-phrase (Lockhart, 2006).

Due to the introduction of FMS attack in 2001 (Fluhrer *et al*, 2001), IEEE 802.11i or WPA2 standard was released in 2004 to replace less secure WEP and WPA. The final IEEE 802.11i standard not only adapts all the improvements included in WPA, but also introduces a new AES-based algorithm considered as fully secure (CPP UK, 2010).

2.3.1 WPA/WPA2 Security Analysis

An improved level of security in WLANs can be implemented using WPA based on a similar acting as WEP. However, does not include most of the flaws of the previous system. The work on the WPA started immediately after the first reports of violation of the WEP and later on was deployed worldwide (Lowe, 2010).

In the article "Don't use WEP for Wi-Fi security" Sayer (2007) measures WPA encryption as a WEP replacement which is more secure and robust to attacks, yet it is able to run on the same hardware than WEP does. Nevertheless, the WPA shared more of the flaws of the WEP. McMillan (2009) concluded that Pre-Shared Keying (PSK) is not secure and short and/or unsecure passwords are almost as disadvantageous as the WEP. Based on similar thesis Takahashi (2004) developed a tool called WPAcrack, a proof of concept which allows a brute force offline dictionary attack against the WPA. Author further concluded that the recommendation of the Wi-Fi alliance to use passwords longer than twenty characters would most likely not be executed in practice by the users of the WPA. Unfortunately, many people do not pay much attention to establishing long passwords and the consequences it may have in the future.

In 2008 security researchers Beck and Tews (2008) announced that they had developed a *"systematic way to partially crack the Wi-Fi Protected Access 2"*. Before this attack, the only other known methods involved a dictionary attack against a weakly chosen pre-shared key. However, the new attack method poses a small threat to WPA2 overall as it does not work against AES – the recommended encryption method for Enterprise Wireless LAN deployments by IEEE and Wi-Fi Alliance (McMillan, 2009).

"There is no weakness in AES or the WPA2 standard based upon it. It's going to last for the next 20 years."

(Robert Graham: Errata Security, 2008)

Kizza (2011) reviews the AES Protocol as *"secure enough to meet the demands Federal Information Standards (FIPS) 140-2"*, which is often demanded by institutions such as Police or Security Agencies. This new algorithm requires a separate chip for the encryption and therefore new hardware is needed (Misic, 2008).

The WPA/WPA2 are also subject to vulnerabilities affecting other 802.11i standard mechanisms such as attacks with 802.1X message spoofing, first described by Arbaugh and Mishra (2001). Furthermore, Kizza (2011) noted that using the WPA2 protocol it does not guarantee protection against attacks such as: frequency jamming, Denial of Service or de-authentication and de-association attacks.

2.3.2 How WPA works

WPA includes two types of user authentication. One named WPA Personal with a pre-shared key mechanism similar to the WEP and the WPA Enterprise, which uses 802.1X and derives its keys (Lockhart, 2006). Nonetheless, the main improvement of the WPA was introduction of Temporal Key Integrity Protocol (TKIP). Instead of using a pre-shared key, which creates a keystream, WPA uses a pre-shared key to serve as the seed for generating the encryption keys (Lammle, 2010).

For data encryption, the WPA uses the RC4 stream cipher with a 128-bit key and a 48-bit IV, which is similar to the WEP. However, unlike the WEP, there is a major improvement for *"WPA to use the Temporal Key Integrity Protocol (TKIP), which the heart of WPA"* (Lammle, 2010). Due to the similarity of the encryption process to the WEP, implementation of the WPA can be as simple as upgrading clients' software and updating the firmware of older access points (Lowe, 2010).

2.3.3 How WPA2 works

Like WPA, WPA2 offers two security modes:

- pre-shared key authentication based on a shared secret,
- authentication by an authentication server

Pre-shared key authentication is intended for personal and small office use where an authentication server is unavailable (Lammle, 2010). Both the WPA and the WPA2 networks use a pre-shared key and are vulnerable to the dictionary attacks (Phifer, 2007). It is significant to make the secret passphrase as long and as casual as possible (at least 20 characters long) with a mix of various random characters (numbers, uppercases etc.) (Lockhart, 2006).

WPA2 also introduces the authentication of Robust Security Network (RSN). *"The RSN enhances the weak security of WEP and provides better protection for the wireless link by allowing the creation of Robust Security Network Associations (RSNA) only"*(Cache and Liu, 2010).

2.3.4 Conclusion

Through the improvements discussed above, WPA and WPA2 successfully provide more secure WLAN and make breaking into the network tougher. There are of course issues with TKIP (similarly to WEP) that allow small packets like ARP to be decrypted, yet there is no way to completely compromise a secure WPA key as well as it can be done with the WEP.

If the WPA is appropriately implemented and sufficiently managed, it will be a very strong security and highly difficult task of breaking; especially with the implementation of the AES-CCMP, which is the most secure wireless network configuration in use today.

2.4.   SSID

A Wireless LAN is identified by its Service Set Identifier (SSID), otherwise known as "Network Name" (Lammle, 2010). It must be shared by an Access point in order to authenticate clients to the network. Nowadays, most of the Access Points allow to "hide" the SSID and regard it as a secret. However, in order to operate the network, the Access Points need to answer clients with the correct SSID and this type of transmitted traffic allows possible attackers to sniff it (Lockhart, 2006). This mechanism therefore can only help to fulfil authentication in WLANs.

2.5.   MAC FILTERING

Every network card is identified by its unique MAC address. Although WLAN standard does not define Access Control, every AP nowadays implements MAC address filtering, often illustrated in the form of a simple list (Kizza, 2011). This mechanism could provide Authenticity, however MAC addresses are not as fixed as they apprear to be. In result the MAC addresses can be forged rather easily (if 'config' under Linux, Registry under Windows). According to Lockhart (2006) an attacker can without difficulty sniff the network traffic to see which stations are communicating in the network and can "choose" one MAC address that is allowed to access the network. He then can change it and access the network. This process is known as MAC spoofing. MAC Filtering should be used only as a small part of the security strategy.

2.6.   VPN

A different approach for securing WLANs is Virtual Private Network (VPN). This term is used to "describe a security system operating at the TCP/IP Layer" (EC-Council, 2009).

Once the flaws of the WEP were examined by Walker (2000) and first attacks were launched by Fluhrer et al. (2001), institutions turned to the VPN as add-on security mechanisms. The two VPN technologies recommended by Dowd (2003), used as an example in this project, are IP Security (IPSec) and Secure Socket Layer (SSL). A strong encryption of IPSec, which is recently mainly used for the VPN, is the safest way to secure access within the AP. VPN with IPsec solution can protect users from the attacks that directly influence the confidentiality of application data but cannot prevent attacks that indirectly ruin confidentiality. Man in the middle, high-jacking and replay attacks are the best examples of these types of attacks. However, the SSL is thought to be a better solution to be used with remote users to connect to private networks as the performance limitation is minimal (Coleman, 2009). In addition, the VPN's were not designed for wireless networks and have a negative effect on the overall throughput, thus Lockhart (2006) proposes the VPN as a good solution if a network already implements the VPN in the wireless network as an addition.

2.7.   WIRELESS LAN ATTACKS

Many of the wireless attack tools are developed to compromise WLAN networks. The popularity and widespread use of WLAN gives the attacker a platform in which they can cause the most trouble. As other technologies gain popularity and practicality, the more attack tools are developed for those technologies.

Cache and Liu's (2010) literature classifies wireless attacks into two main categories:

Passive attacks

- Replay attack
- Eavesdropping
- Brute force
- Brue force dictionary
- Statistical

Active attacks

- Man In the middle
- Denial of Service
- Distributed Denial of Service

Passive attacks are used to collect information like the network SSID, the type of authentication and the type of encryption. Active attacks are used to launch an attack against the wireless network.

2.7.1 Passive Attacks

In these attacks, an unauthorized user acquires access to the network data sources. There is no adjustment of message content, but it is possible to spy on the transmission. *"Passive attacks are meant not to disrupt, but to acquire information flowing across the wireless network"* (Cache and Liu, 2010). The freeware program "inSSIDer" is a popular wireless program that is commonly used to locate wireless networks (Hurley et al, 2007). It can identify the Service Set Identifier (SSID), determine the encryption used, and even determine the manufacturer of the access point. This information is further used by tools such as Airodump-ng to capture required data

2.7.1.1 Replay attack:

In this type of passive attack, the attacker intercepts or eavesdrops on the data channel. The attacker does not do anything to compromise the systems at first, but can resend altered messages to an authorized user pretending to be the system host (Hurley *et al*, 2007).

2.7.1.2 Eavesdropping:

This is a passive attack in which the hacker listens to all the network transmissions in an effort to acquire information travelling from one wireless workstation to the access point.

2.7.1.3 Brute force attacks

These attacks attempt to break the encryption of captured traffic through brute force, trying every possible key combination. A particularly popular type of brute-force attack is the dictionary attack, also called the "offline" dictionary attack (Hurley *et al*, 2007). For example, if the secret passphrase is "sausages," a dictionary attack would attempt different commonly used words in encryption and compare the result with the captured traffic. When there is a match (in this case, "sausages"), the key is cracked.

WPA/WPA2 networks use a pre-shared key which is vulnerable to this attack. In fact, the dictionary attack is the only known cryptographic vulnerability of WPA/WPA2-PSK networks (Aircrack-ng, 2010; Cache and Liu, 2010).

2.7.1.4 Statistical attacks

These attacks exploit flaws in the encryption methods to crack the key from captured traffic. The most widely known static attacks are the WEP attacks FMS, KoReK, and PTW. WPA and WPA2 networks are currently assumed to be immune from these attacks (Aircrack-ng, 2010).

2.7.2 Active Attacks

Active attacks are attacks which not only receive wireless traffic but also transmit wireless traffic, taking an active role in the targeted wireless network. Unauthorized access, spoofing, and denial of service attacks can be considered to be active attacks (EC-Council, 2010). Assuming that the attacker has gained enough information from the passive attack, he can then produce an active attack. In contrast to passive attacks, active attacks can be prevented. (Hurley *et al*, 2007).

2.7.2.1 Denial of Service

Denial of Service attacks attempt to deny service to the users. Over a wireless network, these attacks can be identical to their wired equivalents and include ping floods, ARP attacks, and Distrbuted DoS (DDoS) attacks (Cache and Liu, 2010).Open and WEP secured networks are vulnerable to this denial of- service attacks, as can be easily accessed. Fortunately, WPA/WPA2 based networks are protected from active DoS attacks. However, WPA networks can be vulnerable to another version of the DoS attack. (Howard et al, 2010)

Another form of a denial of service attack is the disconnecting legitimate users by sending false disassociation frames. When the access point receives these frames, it will disconnect the "supposed" sender from the network. (Howard et al, 2010).

2.7.2.2 Man-in-the-middle

Man in the Middle attacks are a class of attacks that set up illegal access points within range of wireless clients for the purpose of acting as a "middle man". (Cache and Liu, 2010). When clients see the rogue access point, the SSID matches the legitimate access point and they mistakenly join it instead of the true access point (Hatch, 2008). Once the attacker is connected to the network can use tools like Ettercap, or other Man-in the-Middle tools to capture sensitive information. (Hurley *et al*, 2007).

3. METHODOLOGY

The main approach used in this project is the comparative approach such as a comparison of the security features and the performance characteristics of different security technologies. Therefore, understanding of the concepts, architectures and practicalities of various WLAN systems and security measures are necessary to ensure the experiment adequacy.

WLAN security was thoroughly researched, explained in the form of the Literature Review and demonstrated in experimental section of this project. Since the WEP has the greatest number of vulnerabilities, the WEP is where the main focus is directed. WPA finds its interest since it replaces the WEP in many circumstances, yet it can still be insecure. Thus, the investigation and testing of WPA and WPAv2 is documented.

The Project has two distinct phases: Research and Practical Experimentation.

3.1 RESEARCH METHODOLOGY

Research area covered a wider range of encryption/authentication methods including the WEP, WPA and the WPA2, to provide a theoretical comparison of their contrasting ability to prevent penetrating. As the WEP has been in the news headlines in the past decade, the information on insecurities of the WEP were easy to find. The WEP was ideal as a case study to explore the reasons of the WEP failure and examples of the solid WLAN securities.

The research findings were refined into a first, rough Project Definition Report (Appendix F). In the next phase a series of questions that needed to be answered in the process of the literature review were developed. Moreover, Project Review report was created (Appendix G) demonstrating the progress made during the previous stages of the final year project, indicating further development and narrowing the research area.

3.2 EXPERIMENTAL METHODOLOGY

The main methodology for producing a final report was based on experiments. This methodology was chosen as the WLAN security can be highly theoretical to understand and explore. By adding practical base to the project, it evolved into enjoyable learning curve that can be applied in the future.

To get an insight into the real-world wireless security statistics, the author attempted to demonstrate that a large number of networks still use inadequate protection by performing a network discovery (wardriving) experiment within a randomly selected area of Southampton City. The findings can be found in Chapter 4.

The next experimental phase of the project simulates breaking the WEP and the WPA encryption and gaining access to a test network. A range of penetration attack strategies were shown and attached within the appendices B, C and D. To minimise the level of difficulty in completing the project, early testing was performed using several Windows and Linux based software tools in early stage of implementation. However, it quickly led to the conclusion that Windows tools are very limited in capabilities. For instance, unless operating in very controlled circumstances, it is nearly impossible to perform packet injection (ARP Replay Attack). According to an extensive research, particularly from Lockhart textbook and the WLAN hacking related forums, an informed decision has been made to perform a penetration attack using Aircrack software suite designed for Linux. Therefore, BackTrack distribution of Linux was used as it includes the most suitable tools to perform the experiments. The results from the experimentation are included in Chapter 5.

3.3.   PLANNING AND MONITORING

A project of this size required a careful and precise planning process, which is illustrated in a Gantt chart (Appendix A). Specific milestones have been indicated on the included Gantt chart to designate successful completion of each phase. Additionally, percentage of task completion was updated so the achievements were clearly visible in the progress of the report and the Gantt chart dictated the plan for the next period.

In order to compensate for the unpredictable occurrences, the plan included a contingency time of an extra day every two weeks. Extra time was absolutely essential to the progress of the project.

To keep an updated log of the process a log book was used. This helped to focus on the project and keep track of the progression. Particularly useful were mind maps and personal notes allowing greater precision and exploration of ideas from a variety of angles.

Following the theoretical research, the author dedicated time to conducting initial practical experimentation. This enabled the author to have a better understanding of the time that would likely be required to complete each stage.

Although not anticipated in the original plan it quickly became apparent that the author has underestimated the level of skills required and the complexity of the Linux Operating System.

It had an impact on the overall time scale of the project. The time was consumed to solve issues with hardware compatibility in terms of driver availability influencing the choice of specific OS distribution.

At the end of the project, the motivation levels were quite low. To counter this problem a checklist was used. It contained all tasks that still needed to be done divided into must haves, should haves and could haves. Every time a task was finished, it was crossed out and the more tasks were crossed out the higher was the motivation.

3.4. RISK ASSESSMENT

Several risk factors were assessed in early stage of the project in order to compensate unpredictable issues with implementation and testing.

Complexity

- Performing several tasks, including Packet Injection, during the practical phase may require more time than anticipated as very specific network conditions are needed.
    - To compensate for this, considerable research has been performed and many technical resources have been identified.

Compatibility

- Despite significant research, a potential issue could still arise from compatibility between the chosen operating system and some of the acquired software tools. This may only become obvious at the time of use.
    - To compensate, there is a variety of choice amongst Linux OS distributions. Windows based testing is also a possibility.

Equipment Failure

- The project depends upon reliable operation of a specialist wireless network card which is only available via mail order. The impact of equipment failure could result in up to a week of lost time.
    - To compensate, the author has acquired another suitable but not identical wireless network card

3.5. CONCLUSION

There were several expected outcomes hoped to be achieved as a result of using this method and approach. The research approach aimed to raise the awareness of security issues, especially those related to the wireless LAN security. It is suggested that a reader will understand that every technology has its flaws and vulnerabilities, and often it is up to the users of technology to be aware and take actions to rectify and to use these technologies consequently.

4. WIRELESS NETWORK SECURITY SURVEY: WARDRIVING

4.1.   INTRODUCTION

Hurley *et al* (2007) describe Wardriving as *"the act of moving around a specific area and mapping the population of wireless access points for statistical purposes"*. These statistics are then used to raise awareness of the security problems. The term Wardriving has been coined by Peter M. Shipley, who was the first to automate the process of Wardriving in 2001 (Hurley et al, 2004). In his observations of the San Francisco Bay Area he found only 15-30 per cent of the Access Points to be encrypted.

In this chapter data collected by the author is analysed. The aim is to demonstrate the security awareness of WLANs in Southampton area. In the first section, the methodology used to capture and analyse the data is discussed. In the following sections, the data is analysed and finally conclusions are given.

4.2.   METHODOLOGY

Data was captured by conducting a wardrive and capturing available WLANS in randomly chosen area of Southampton using a powerful wardriving tool, inSSIDer (Figure 1).

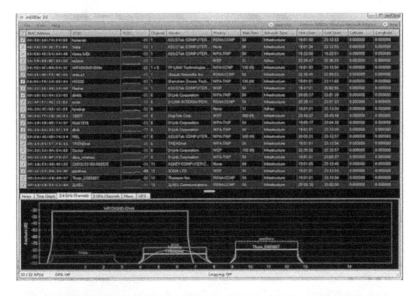

Figure 4-1. InSSIDer Main Window (Screenshot taken during experimentation)

Data was collected using a laptop equipped with the wireless network card and antenna. InSSIDer was actively searching for available wireless networks, giving significant information: the name of the SSID, the standard 802.11 b, g or n connection type (infrastructure or ad hoc), signal strength, noise level, and perhaps most importantly - security level (none or WEP / WPA / WPA2). However, it did not show whether the MAC filtration is applied. Research was conducted in a car with a computer positioned on the passenger seat. In later stage of the experiment the author acquired an Alfa External Network card and USB GPS device which allowed for more precise collection of data as it contain high gain omnidirectional antenna.

4.3. FINDINGS

The table below illustrates the results of a number of studies on the WLAN security networks level found. The results of these studies were varied. Nevertheless, the amount of unsecured or poorly secured wireless networks is high in each case.

Place	Year	Number of networks found	Unsecured	WEP	WPA/ WPA2	Source
Los Angeles	2002	580	70%	30%	N/A	Wi-Foo Book
Paris	2006	1000	29.5%	66%	5%	Kaspersky Lab www.viruslist.pl
London	2007	800	35%	49%	16	Kaspersky Lab www.viruslist.pl
Kracov	2007	1449	40%	46%	17%	Kaspersky Lab www.viruslist.pl
Lublin	2010	2100	19.4%	16.6%	64%	Kaspersky Lab www.viruslist.pl

Figure 4-2. Wardriving results from different sources

The author decided to conduct similar research in the area of Southampton to compare the results of studies.

4.4. RESULTS

The author collected data of the 348 access points illustrated in the findings below.

Place	Year	Number of networks found	Unsecured	WEP	WPA/ WPA2
Southampton	2011	348	10.3%	28.8%	60.9% (212)

Figure 4-3. Wardriving Results

Percentage based pie graph was created to illustrate the results transparently.

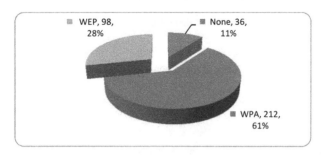

Figure 4-4. Pie-chart - wardriving results breakdown

From all of the access points found, 308 (89.7%) were protected with the WEP or the WPA encryption and 36 (10.3%) did not have any security. This is a major improvement in comparison to previous years, yet another issue can be concluded form the findings. 29% of users still use the WEP encryption – method considered as out of date and unsecure.

60.9% of the users use the WPA or the WPA2 algorithm, which is certainly safer than the WEP. The security level strongly relies on the person that sets up the access point. The strength of protection depends on the length and the quality of the password.

The tool InSSIDer was able to save the coordinates aquired by the GPS unit, introduced in later stages of the survey, It was then transferred to Google Maps application. The figure below illustrates the geographical image of the encryption used in the area of Southampton. The access point names were hidden due to the confidentiality issue.

Green Color: Unsecured   Yellow Color: WEP   Pink Color: WPA   Red   Color: WPA2

Figure 4-5. Geographical implementation of wardriving results

4.5.   Conclusions

The chart below illustrates the amount of access points with the actual security versus the amount of people with none or very weak security (WEP).

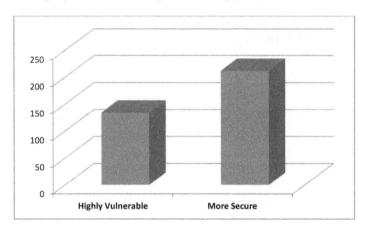

Figure 4-6. Chart: Highly Vulnerable vs More Secure access points .

The results illustrate that almost 40 per cent of the networks are highly vulnerable and easily accessible to the attackers, whereas remaining 60 per cent are more secure, yet not fully secure. Findings immediately raise a concern that even after nine years of the WEP protocol in use and officially considered as 'leaky', users continue to take a little notice of the issues associated after the break in. It becomes effortless to intercept private communications, view visited web sites, logins and passwords. Moreover, neighbours can get a free broadband access to the Internet, and mobile users can get free Internet almost anywhere in the area.

5. WIRELESS LAN PENETRATION TESTS

5.1.   INTRODUCTION

A Wireless LAN Penetration Test is not much different from a normal hack, however the main difference is that the owners of attacked WLAN are previously informed about the situation, and they agree to it. This type of testing is widely used by the ethical hackers to assess the security of wireless networks.

To minimise the difficulties in completing this experiment, initial testing was performed using several Windows based software tools. However, it quickly led to the conclusion that Windows tools are very limited in capabilities. For example, unless operating in very controlled circumstances, it is nearly impossible to perform packet injection (ARP Replay Attack).

5.2.   METHODOLOGY

All network sniffing and penetration testing documented in this report was conducted with the following set up:

Acer Travelamte 8000 1.8 GHz CPU Laptop with 1 GB RAM

Linux Bactrack Distributon – Live CD

Wireless card supporting monitoring mode – Alfa AWUS036

Windows is not optional for the WLAN penetration tests due to the number of the wireless cards having driver compatibility issues. Moreover, installing Linux can be quite tricky, thus a Linux Live CD was considered. Fortunately, there is a special distribution for WLAN penetration tests called Backtrack.

BackTrack has a long history and it was based on several different Linux distributions. Nowadays it is based on a Slackware Linux distribution and the corresponding live- CD scripts by Tomas M. (SLAX, 2011). Each package, configuration and script is optimized to be used by security penetration testers. Currently *"BackTrack consists of more than 300 tools ready, different and updated"*, which are logically structured according the job requirements. New technologies and testing techniques are combined into Backtrack immediately (BackTrack Linux, 2011). The most updated version of Backtrack is second release of version 4 (BackTrack Linux 4 R2).

The ease of the WEP and the WPA cracking can be seen by using tools such as Aircrack suite included in Backtrack distro, which contain estimated 15 different tools, but only four of them are used in the phases of these attacks:

- Airmon – used to put wireless chipset into monitor mode (RFMON)
- Airodump - sniffer tool used to detect WEP/WPA/WPA2-enabled networks,
- Aireplay - a tool to inject packets, also de-authenticate
- Aircrack - a tool used to decrypt pre-shared key

5.3.   CRACKING WEP PASSWORD

The process of breaking into WEP secured network is divided into two experimentations. First test was performed in controlled environment where author has set up the network secured by the 64bit WEP protocol with basic settings and then attempted to penetrate the network using Backtrack Linux Tools.

The goal of the second experiment was to crack a WLAN secured with WEP protocol but this time the author used the access point of his neighbour which agreed to share his network for the time of the experiment. Apart from knowing that the network will be secured with the WEP protocol the author had no more information about additional security settings applied by the neighbour.

The WEP penetration in both tests was performed by active attack meaning the network was flooded with ARP packets to generate traffic. It allowed quicker collection of data and significantly speeded up the process of the whole experiment. "A step by step guide to breaking WEP" diagram (Appendix E), provided by Wirelessdefence.org (2006) allowed monitoring each phase of the attack and ensured the author that the accurate steps are followed.

The wireless adapter used to perform packet injection was Alfa AWUS036H. It features a Realtek 8187L chipset, which is well supported by Linux and gives very good results during penetration tests (Aircrack-ng, 2010). Moreover, included in BackTrack Linux drivers allow simultaneously capturing and injecting packets on the same card. This is called Monitoring or RFMON mode. The process of breaking into WEP secured networks is documented in Appendices B and C.

5.3.1 Results

The amount of time it takes to break into the WEP encrypted wireless network is dependent upon the volume of traffic. Low or lack of network traffic on the Access Point would consume a significant amount of time to collect sufficient Initialisation Vectors and allow cracking to the WEP key. However, there is a method of invoking the Access Point by exchanging packets with the wireless card. This is carried out in an ARP Replay Attack. In result a great amount of network traffic is generated, and subsequently increases packet collection.

To crack the WEP key for an access point a large amount of initialization vectors (IVs) were needed to be gathered. Normal network traffic does not typically generate these IVs in a high speed. It is suggested that about 50 000 IV packets is essential, thus aireplay-ng played major role injecting the traffic in the form of ARP requests. Having generated enough data and captured the IV packets, it was a matter of seconds when Aircrack correctly decrypt my 64bit WEP key in both tests (Figure 5-1).

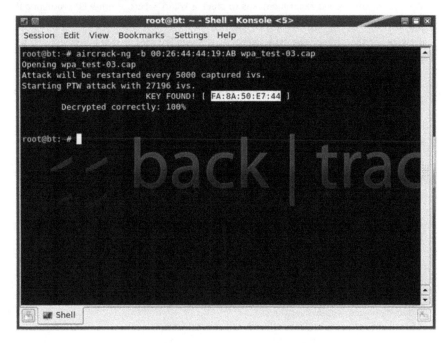

Figure 5-1: Result of successful WEP password crack

However, in the second test (Appendix C) the laptop did not want to associate with the Access Point. Thus, it was concluded that a MAC filtering has been set by the neighbour. Getting past such a filter turned out to be much more trivial than expected. With the additional research it was found that it would easily get the MAC address of stations already connected to the network, then spoof it and use single disassociation attack to disconnect the users form the access point. Afterwards the author was enabled to connect to the network with spoofed MAC address. Accompanied by Linux, MAC spoofing is effortless and supported, thus whole procedure took less than 2 minutes - so much for the security of MAC filters. After entering all the commands required it enabled the author to surf the Internet and the penetration test was successfully completed (Figure 5-2).

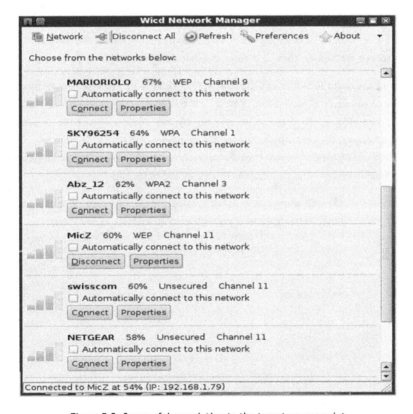

Figure 5-2: Successful association to the target access point

Other attacks could have been employed as the author was inside the network e.g.: packet sniffers. Ethereal is one of the best packet sniffers around so with its help, interesting packets can easily be found. Moreover, with the aid of SSLStrip script (also available in Backtrack) it would enable the author to sniff the passwords and logins entered into popular browsers.

5.3.2 Conclusion

The penetration test was a useful practical application of all the theory that was needed to understand what is happening in the wireless network and identify the security problems. The test showed just how insecure the WEP is, even when it is supported by a MAC filter. From zero knowledge to a working, free internet connection in less than 1 hour that is somehow alarming. Even more terrifying is the fact that it can probably be done in less than 10 minutes and that is NOT secured by anyone's standard.

Without any doubt it can be said that the WEP is "dead" and that it should not be used as the single security mechanism in WLANs. If the WEP is combined with MAC access lists and a hidden SSID it should be able to stop malicious hackers, however against serious hackers, the WPA with a long and secure password is a must. If more security is required the VPN and a firewall implementation is needed. However, this often requires additional hardware what relates to an extra cost and complicated set up.

It is clear that the WEP encryption does not provide sufficient wireless network security and can only be used with higher-level encryption solutions (such as the VPNs).

5.4.   CRACKING WPA PASSWORD

The WEP can be cracked with a relative ease, on the other hand it is not as quick/easy as it is to crack the WPA encrypted network. The difference is that unlike the WEP sessions, which are always crackable, the outcome of the WPA crack is not guaranteed. The main limitation is the length of the pre-shared key. According to Lockhart (2006), since the pre-shared key can be from 8 to 63 characters in length, it effectively becomes impossible to crack the pre-shared key. The only time the pre-shared key can be cracked if it is a dictionary word or relatively short in length.

5.4.1 Results

Having set up the WPA network with 8 character ordinary password (*'sausages'*), the Aircrack suite was used. For the WPA decryption Aircrack needs a dictionary file to "guess" the key. The one used was the basic word lists which contained about 800000 keys (Figure 5-3) .The issue here was an exclusion of the generated key (*'sausages'*), so it was known that finding the key was impossible. Nevertheless, by editing the dictionary and inputting the password known to examine the outcome, it did identify correctly the exact word of the password in the dictionary. The whole process of finding the key in this dictionary took 1 hour and 16 minutes (Figure 5-4)

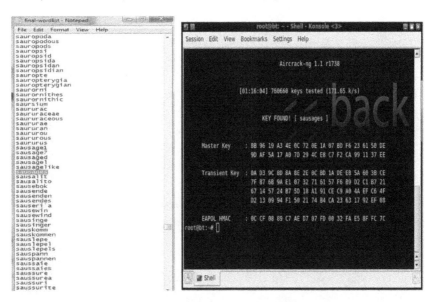

Figure 5-3: Wordlist   example   Figure 5-4 Successful WPA crack

This example provided a test using a previously known password. To successfully crack a random network, an attacker must have a large dictionary file, a powerful computer and a little bit of luck in order to obtain the password. Fortunately, this is not as easy as it sounds.

Another method of cracking pre-shared key is called *brute force attack*, due to a high intensity of the computer to find the key. One computer using this method can only test 50 to 300 possible keys per second depending on the computer's CPU (Central Processing Unit).

According to the LastBit (2011), there are 208,827,064,576 possible ways to create the minimum eight-letter password. The same resource provided a simple calculator available to assess the performance and time of cracking keys with *brute force* method.

During experimentation it was found that the laptop was able to process 170 keys per second. Assuming that a 170 words per second can be tested by one CPU, it might take even 40 years to find the password according to the calculator (Figure below)

Available: http://lastbit.com/pswcalc.asp

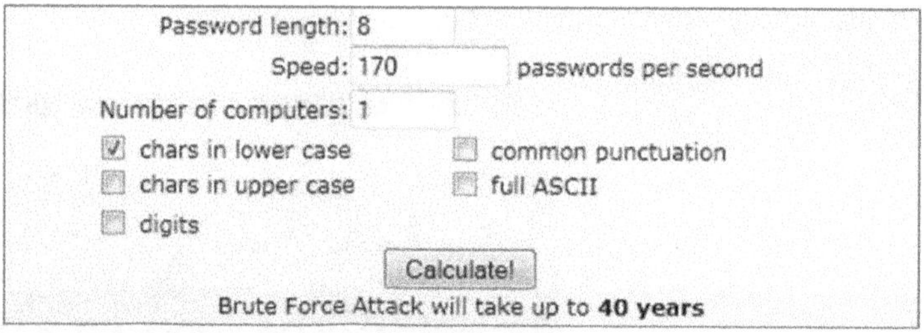

Figure 5-5. Brute force calculator (8 characters password)

(LastBit, 2011),

http://lastbit.com/pswcalc.asp

Even if the hacker has a high performance cluster based supercomputer that can check one million words per second, he may still need a couple of days and realise that the passphrase is not as simple as "12345678"

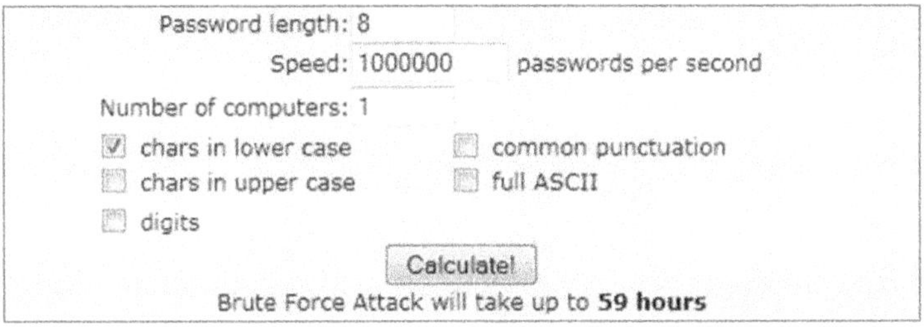

```
Password length: 8
          Speed: 1000000       passwords per second
Number of computers: 1
  ☑ chars in lower case        ☐ common punctuation
  ☐ chars in upper case        ☐ full ASCII
  ☐ digits
                    [ Calculate! ]
     Brute Force Attack will take up to 59 hours
```

Figure 5-6. Brute force calculator (1M keys per second)

(LastBit, 2011),

The situation dramatically changes when password length is increased or digits are added to *brute force* analysis. Using the same powerful machine when password is increased only by two characters it automatically increases the time needed to brute force the key (Figure 5-7)

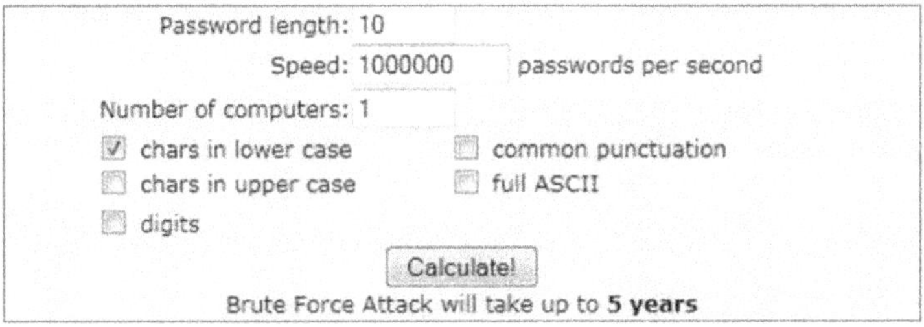

```
Password length: 10
          Speed: 1000000       passwords per second
Number of computers: 1
  ☑ chars in lower case        ☐ common punctuation
  ☐ chars in upper case        ☐ full ASCII
  ☐ digits
                    [ Calculate! ]
     Brute Force Attack will take up to 5 years
```

Figure 5-7. Brute force calculator (10 character key, 1M keys per second)

(LastBit, 2011),

Finally, 20 characters key is widely considered as medium security password. Such a password can be custom ('*sausagessausagessaus*') or generated using Key generators. Generated key usually looks like this: -R+a$oNzqYPe8pn2/2$F and amount of time required to crack such a complicated passwords is "infinite" (Figure 5-8).

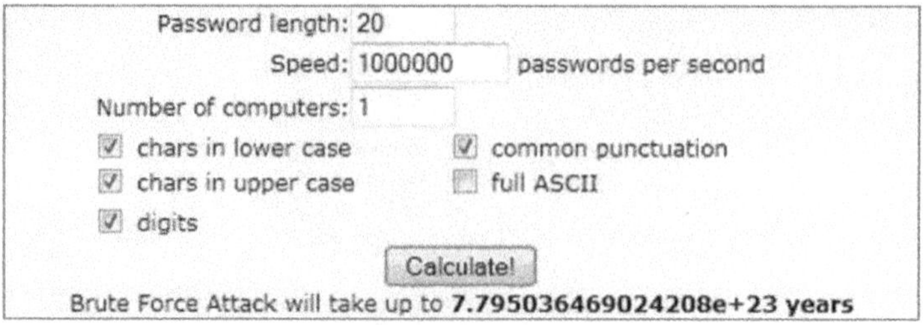

Password length: 20
Speed: 1000000　　passwords per second
Number of computers: 1
☑ chars in lower case　　☑ common punctuation
☑ chars in upper case　　☐ full ASCII
☑ digits

Calculate!

Brute Force Attack will take up to **7.795036469024208e+23 years**

Figure 5-8. Brute force calculator (20 character key, 1M keys per second)

(LastBit, 2011),

5.4.2 Conclusions

The only time the pre-shared key can be cracked is if it is a dictionary word or relatively short in length. Equally, if there is a need for the unbreakable wireless network at home, the use of WPA/WPA2 and a 20 character password composed of random characters including special symbols is essential. If a weak passphrase is used and it is included in the dictionary file, it takes no more than two hours to crack the key. However, depending on the capacity of the dictionary, it can take hours or days to break through large dictionary (millions of keys).

6. RECOMMENDATIONS

Although wireless networks will probably never be completely secure as the research on the protocol vulnerabilities will always continue. The best method is to update on the latest encryption schemes and other network security related items to keep the network secure. The administrator will not be able to stop the sniffing attacks; however, can prevent the attacker from being able to decipher the traffic. Moreover, even the latest security methods have their weaknesses. For instance, WPA2 the latest encryption method, does not address the problem of dissociation and de-authentication attacks, but does address many of the issues with the WEP.

The following countermeasures should help in securing network against casual access, but offer no real protection against more skilled intruders. Based upon the results from the research efforts and experimentation, following guidance is proposed.

1) Change Default Settings of the Access Point

At minimum, change the administration password, and default SSID on AP or wireless router.

2) Enable Encryption and set strong password

Always use either the WPA or the WPA2 encryption when possible. If using the WPA with a pre-shared key, use a strong password; hackers can use dictionary attacks and they will be quite effective a password is simple. You may want to use a strong password generator like the one at *www.grc.com*.

3) Disable SSID broadcasting

If the access point supports it, it is required to consider disabling wireless SSID broadcast; however, this may raise some issues with the APs clients recognising it. (inSSIDer will still recognize it) When changing the SSID, do not use any personal information. Naming a wireless network after a business or a family name is not a wise idea. Attackers could use the SSID to determine who the network belongs to and with more effort, could determine possible weaknesses (Cache and Liu, 2010)

4) Enable MAC address filtering

Many routers will allow filtering clients that can access the network; this is known as Wireless MAC Filtering. If the MAC clients' addresses are known, it can be entered into configuration utility as "Permit". This is not a 100 per cent effective method; MAC addresses can be spoofed to match the AP's associated clients, but it does provide the user with a slightly higher level of security. In large organisations it is recommended to consider implementing Access Control List (ACL) – much more complicated, yet introduces high level of security.

5) Access Point Upgrade: Firmware or Hardware

Having the most current firmware installed on your AP can sometimes help improve security. Updated firmware often includes security bug fixes and sometimes adds new security features. If AP's latest firmware does not support at least the improved security of WPA and preferably WPA2, upgrading to new access point should be taken into consideration (Kizza, 2011).

6) Implement VPN

If you cannot use WPA2 or WPA because the client does not support these encryption and authentication types, a VPN is the next best solution for securing the wireless networks. A VPN combined with IP Security (IPSec) and Secure Sockets Layer (SSL) provide a similar level of security as WPA and WPA2

7) Implement Wireless Intrusion Detection System (WIDS)

The use of wireless IDSs and other network monitors are yet another way to improve the security of the WLAN. A WIDS will provide warnings through the use of alarms which are triggered when the wireless security rules are broken. These alerts allow for real time monitoring and response to unusual activity on the WLAN, however this method is the most expensive as it contains special hardware to be implemented (Cache and Liu, 2010).

7. PROJECT EVALUATION

7.1   EVALUATION OF THE OBJECTIVES

The most important objective was to expand the knowledge of the wireless LAN security. The content of the report delivers set objectives. However, more advanced security mechanisms like the WPA2 Enterprise and the VPN would make a good project addition. It is an important topic as authentication is a major issue in corporate and university WLANs. Further reading on the WPA2 Enterprise and the VPN technologies would have broaden the project to the extent not visible within the time scale.

Another objective was to examine how WLANs can be made more secure. When the security protocols have been explored in this paper, they have been further evaluated for their practical use. WLAN penetration test was performed to test the knowledge I already possess and to get more practical experience. The objective was achieved to a greater extent in the experimental part, where the security idea was expanded to include WPA/WPA2 penetration tests. It is relatively easy to hack into a WLAN with tools that can be downloaded from the Internet. No big intellectual challenge in doing such tests is required as books and tutorials available cover this issue. Most of them in detail describe the WLAN basics and give instructions on how to use the tools available, therefore the step by step process of doing the tests was only documented as appendices and the actual results have been put to the main body of this project. The practical part was enjoyable and provided enough insight to at least partially cover this objective.

7.2   EVALUATION OF THE METHODOLOGY

The experiments conducted in this project have been found as partially reliable and fit for its purpose. The hacking experiments were 100 per cent successful and allowed to generate decent comparisons and conclusions, however the wardriving survey has not met the expectations in full. The findings focused only on encryption methods, where more security issues could have been taken into consideration and critically explored.

The original intentions in regards to this study were highly demanding. Unfortunately, the more advanced the project was the tougher it became to meet the demands due to a timescale and not efficient enough collection of secondary data. Literature review focused too strongly on the theoretical background of encryption methods rather than including other technologies that could have been implemented. Further experiments conducted became a challenge to critically explore in comparison to the current data acquired. Nevertheless, the tests proved that it is possible to hack to other networks with little effort. Security networks are still associated with many issues that individuals and business take for granted. This project exposed those issues and illustrated the effortless approach to acquiring information from other users. What became an advantage was the choice of Linux as a base for the penetration experiments, allowing additional knowledge, simultaneously achieving a personal goal.

With projects like this there is always a room for improvements. Despite well organised project plan, perhaps the time could have been used even more efficiently. Preparation for the supervisory meetings could have generated more to the point questions, which would have improved the collection of secondary data. The time spent on research and Linux complexity carried away the author from the core of the project impacting the quality of the data.

The original plan has been amended after the collection of data and its analysis. It became difficult as the data gathered was a good base for technological and security comparisons, yet the literature did not specify a wider range of solutions. On the other hand, too broad selection could take away the focus on the objectives and lead to lack of clarity.

7.3   REFLECTION

At the beginning of the project, not much thought had been given on using methodology at all. It was mainly learning by doing. Many things could have been done better or more efficient. A lot of time was spent on focussing on unimportant things like the formatting while this time should have been better spent on reading and selecting methodologies. The Gantt chart for instance, was seen as unnecessary, but it really proved to be helpful once the project was in more advance stage. The satisfaction of finishing a chapter to the deadline kept motivation and drive to completion.

As the project required a lot of work, it needed to get used to working on time planning of some sort. Normal assignments can usually be done in a few days and can easily be split into a few tasks. The project however requires constant work and this requires continuous planning and control therefore

The WLAN penetration test was probably the best moments in the project process. It was nice to put the theory to work and see just how flawed WEP and WPA really is.

One of the most challenging tasks in completing this test was finding the right wireless LAN card that would work using aircrack-ng under Linux operating system. Once the right wireless LAN card has been found, cracking the WEP was simple and easy to do.

Despite the issues encountered, the overall project is seen by the author as a great learning curve and skills development in the area of wireless security. The project generated a greater understanding of the Wireless security technologies, which can be potentially used for the future reference. The author found the feedback from the supervisor useful, therefore any constructive criticism was applied to the project and reflected upon.

The overall, project has been a challenging task, however the research of LAN security explored in detail potential issues associated with security confirmed by the experiments conducted. The objectives were thoroughly discussed and proved that current security of WLANs although improved, still require more attention. The consequences of breaking into other networks may carry serious damages therefore recommendations have been made.

8. REFERENCES

1. Abdalla, M., Pointcheval, D., Fouque, P. A. & Vergnaud, D. 2009. Applied Cryptography and Network Security: 7th International Conference, ACNS 2009, Paris-Rocquencourt, France, June 2-5, 2009, Proceedings, Springer.

2. Aircrack-ng. 2010. Compaibility Drivers. [online] Available http://www.aircrack-ng.org/doku.php?id=compatibility_drivers [accessed 10 January 2011]

3. Alfa Network. 2010. Product description: AWUS036H. [online]. Available: http://www.alfa.com.tw/in/front/bin/ptdetail.phtml?Part=AWUS036NH&Category=10 5463 [accessed 10 January 2011]

4. Arbaugh, W., Mishra, A., 2001."An Initial Security Analysis of the 802.1X Standard [online] Avaialble: http://www.cs.umd.edu/%7Ewaa/1x.pdf [[accessed 30th January 2011].

5. BackTrack Linux., 2011. About [online] Available: http://www.backtrack-linux.org/about/ [accessed 4 January 2011]

6. Barken, L. et.al. 2004. Wireless Hacking: Projects for Wi-Fi Enthusiasts. Syngress

7. Bayles, A. W. & Hurley, C. 2007. Penetration Tester's Open Source Toolkit, Syngress Publishing.

8. Beaver, K. & McClure, S. 2010. Hacking For Dummies, John Wiley & Sons.

9. Beaver. K. and Davis, P. 2005. Hacking Wireless Networks for Dummies. Wiley: Indianapolis

10. Beck. M. and Tews. E., 2008. Practical attacks against WEP and WPA [online] Available: http://dl.aircrack-ng.org/breakingwepandwpa.pdf [accessed 19 April 2011]

11. Bel., 2009. DATA ENCRYPTION, ENABLING AUTHENTICATION AND WIRELESS SECURITY [online]. Available: http://beautbelsblog.wordpress.com/2009/10/25/data-encryption-enabling-authentication-and-wireless-security/ [accessed 19 April 2011].

12. Borisov, N., Goldberg, I., and Wagner, D. (2001) Intercepting Mobile Communications: The Insecurity of 802.11 [online] Available: http://www.cs.berkeley.edu/~daw/papers/wep-mob01.pdf [accessed 15th December 2010]

13. Briere, D., Hurley, P. & Ferris, E. 2010. Wireless Home Networking For Dummies, John Wiley & Sons.

14. Burns, B. 2007. Security power tools, O'Reilly.

15. Cache. J and Liu V., 2010. Hacking Exposed Wireless: Wireless Security Secrets & Solutions - - McGraw-Hill Education

16. Cisco Support., 2008. [online]. Available:
    https://supportforums.cisco.com/thread/342246 [accessed 19 April 2011].

17. Cisco. 2001, Cisco Aironet Security Solution Provides Dynamic WEP to Address
    Researchers' Concerns, [online]], http://www.securitytechnet.com/resource/rsc-
    center/vendor-wp/cisco/1281_pp.pdf [accessed 30th April 2006]

18. Coleman, D. D., Westcott, D. A., Harkins, B. E. & Jackman, S. M. 2009. CWSP:
    Certified Wireless Security Professional Official Study Guide, John Wiley & Sons.

19. CPP UK., 2010. National Identity Fraud Prevention Week Study conducted by Hart
    Jason [online video]. Available:
    http://www.youtube.com/watch?v=JRfxzMl4dPw&feature=player_embedded
    [accessed 15 January 2011]

20. Dowd, T., 2003. Secure the network the same as a home: basic rules apply to keeping
    unwanted visitors out of prized possessions at home and at work. [online]
    Communications News, April 2003, v40 i4, p32 (1) Available: Academic One File
    Database

21. EC-Council 2009a. Wireless Safety: Wireless5 Safety Certification, COURSE
    TECHNOLOGY.

22. EC-Council 2010. Penetration Testing: Network Threat Testing, Course Technology.

23. EC-Council. 2009b. Secure Network Infrastructures, COURSE TECHNOLOGY.

24. Errata Security., 2008. News [online] Available:
    http://www.erratasec.com/news.html [accessed 17 December 2010]

25. Flickenger, R. & Weeks, R. 2006. Wireless hacks, O'Reilly.

26. Fluhrer, S., Mantin, I. and Shamir, S.2001. Weaknesses in the Key Scheduling
    Algorithm of RC4 [online].Available:
    http://www.crypto.com/papers/others/rc4_ksaproc.pdf [accessed 30th November
    2010]

27. Gast, Mathew S. 2005, 802.11 Wireless Networks The Definitive Guide (2nd edn.), USA,
    O'Reilly, Seabastopol

28. Hatch, B. 2008. Hacking exposed Linux: Linux security secrets & solutions, McGraw-
    Hill.

29. Howard, D. & Prince, K. 2010. Security 2020: Reduce Security Risks This Decade, John
    Wiley & Sons.

30. Howard, R., Graham, J. & Olson, R. 2010. Cyber Security Essentials, Auerbach
    Publishers, Incorporated.

31. Hurley, C, et.al. 2007. WarDriving and Wireless Penetration Testing Syngress: Canada

32. Hurley, C. & Thornton, F. 2004. WarDriving: drive, detect, defend : a guide to wireless security, Syngress.
33. I.S.S.W.G., 2011. Information Systems Security Working Group: Security? [online]. Avaialable: http://www.isswg.org.uk/cia.php [accessed 15 April 2011]
34. IEEE-SA Standards Board., 2001. 802.11b [online] Available: http://standards.ieee.org/getieee802/download/802.11b-1999.pdf [accessed 30 January 2011]
35. IEEE-SA Standards Board., 2001. 802.11d [online] Available: http://standards.ieee.org/getieee802/download/802.11d-2001.pdf [accessed 30 January 2011]
36. IEEE-SA Standards Board., 2003. 802.11g [online] Available: http://standards.ieee.org/getieee802/download/802.11g-2003.pdf [accessed 30 January 2011]
37. IEEE-SA Standards Board., 2003. 802.11h [online] Available: http://standards.ieee.org/getieee802/download/802.11h-2003.pdf [accessed 30 January 2011]
38. IEEE-SA Standards Board., 2004. 802.11i [online] Available: http://standards.ieee.org/getieee802/download/802.11i-2004.pdf [accessed 30 January 2011].
39. IEEE-SA Standards Board., 2004. 802.1X [online] Available: http://standards.ieee.org/getieee802/download/802.1X-2004.pdf [accessed 1 February 2011]
40. IEEE-SA Standards Board.,1999. 802.11 [online] Available: http://standards.ieee.org/getieee802/download/802.11-1999.pdf [accessed 30th January 2011].
41. IEEE-SA Standards Board.,1999. 802.11a [online] Available: http://standards.ieee.org/getieee802/download/802.11a-1999.pdf [accessed 30th January 2011]
42. Kizza, J. M. 2011. Computer Network Security and Cyber Ethics, McFarland & Co Inc Pub.
43. Krishnan, S. P. T., Veeravalli, B. & Wong, L. W. C. 2008. Wireless LANs (WLANs): Security and Privacy. Encyclopedia of Wireless and Mobile Communications, 1392 - 1406.
44. Kumkum, G. 2010. Mobile Computing: Theory and Practice, Pearson Education.
45. Lammle, T. 2010. CCNA Wireless Study Guide: IUWNE Exam 640-721, John Wiley & Sons.

46. Lockhart, A., 2006. Network security hacks. 2nd ed.. Sebastopol, CA: O'Reilly

47. Lowe, D. 2010. Networking All-in-One For Dummies, John Wiley & Sons.

48. McMillan. R., 2009. Network World. "New Attack Cracks Common Wi-Fi Encryption in a Minute: Attack Works on Older WPA Systems That Use the TKIP Algorithm." [online]. Available: http://www.networkworld.com/news/2009/082709-new-attackcracks-common-wi-fi.html [accessed 5 January 2011].

49. Misic, J.and Misic, V. 2008. Wireless Personal Area Networks : Performance, Interconnection, and Security with IEEE 802. 15. 4. Wiley-Interscience:Chichester :

50. Raggi, E., Thomas, K., Channelle, A., Parsons, T. & Vugt, S. 2010. Beginning Ubuntu Linux, Fifth Edition, Apress.

51. REFERENCES:

52. Sayer. P.,2007. Don't use WEP for Wi-Fi security. Computerworld [online] Available: http://www.computerworld.com/s/article/9015559/Don_t_use_WEP_for_Wi_Fi_securi ty_researchers_say [accessed 11 January 2011]

53. Simpson, M. T., Backman, K. & Corley, J. 2010. Hands-On Ethical Hacking and Network Defense, Cengage Learning.

54. SLAX, 2011. Feedback.[online] Available: http://www.slax.org [Accessed 4 January 2011]

55. Takahashi, T. 2004, WPA Passive Dictionary Attack Overview [online] Available: http://www.tinypeap.com/docs/WPA_Passive_Dictionary_Attack_Overview.pdf [accessed 20 November 2010]

56. Tews,E., Weinmann,R., Pyshkin.A., 2007. Breaking 104 bit wep in less than 60 seconds.[Online] Avaialable: http://eprint.iacr.org/2007/120.pdf [accessed 15 November 2010]

57. Vladimirov, A. A., Gavrilenko, K. V. & Mikhailovsky, A. A. 2004. Wi-Foo, Addison-Wesley.

58. Vladimirov.A, Konstantin. V, Gavrilenko. A,.2010. Wi-Foo, The Secrets of Wireless Hacking. Addison-Wesley Buch

59. Walker, J. R. 2000. Unsafe at any key size; an analysis of the WEP encapsulation."IEEE Document 802.11-00/362 [online]. Available: http://grouper.ieee.org/groups/802/11/Documents/index.html document [accessed 7 January 2011]

60. Wi-Fi Alliance. 2003. Securing Wi-Fi Wireless Networks with Today's Technologies [security whitepaper] http://www.wifi.org/files/uploaded_files/wp_4_Securing%20Wireless%20Networks_2-6-03.pdf [accessed 30th February 2011]

61. Wirelessdefence.org, 2006. A step by step guide to breaking WEP [online]. Available: http://wirelessdefence.org/Contents/802.11%20Basics.htm [accessed 19 November 2010]

62. Zhang, Y., Zheng, J. & Ma, M. 2008. Handbook of research on wireless security, Information Science Reference.

9. APPENDICES

9.1 Appendix A: Gantt Chart

9.2 Appendix B: Cracking WEP Password: Initial experimentation

9.3 Appendix C: Cracking WEP Password: Final experimentation

9.4 Appendix D: Cracking WPA Password

9.5 Appendix E: Diagram: WEP Step by step

9.6 Appendix F: Project Definition Report

9.7 Appendix G: Project Review Report

9.8 Appendix H: Ethics Release

9.1.   APPENDIX A

PROJECT GANTT CHART

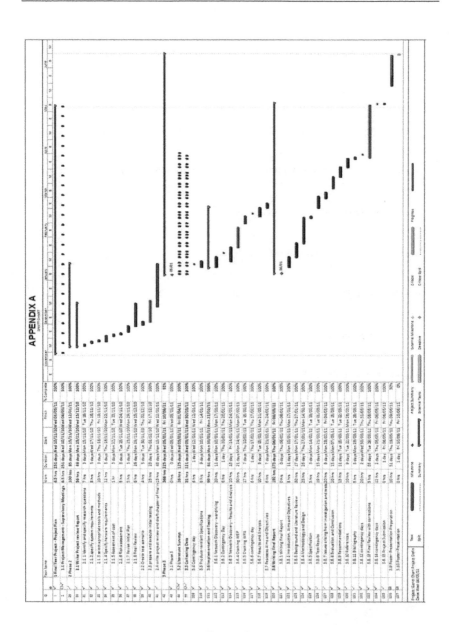

9.2. APPENDIX B

INITIAL EXPERIMENT: CRACKING WEP PASSWORD

This initial experimentation uses the Aircrack suite of utilities (airmon-ng, airodump-ng, aireplay-ng and aircrack-ng), in Backtrack 4

First of all general scan for the target Access Point need to be performed to collect the BSSID and Wireless Channel that the Access Point is using, as this will be required later.

To perform a general scan, following command must be entered:

airodump-ng mon0

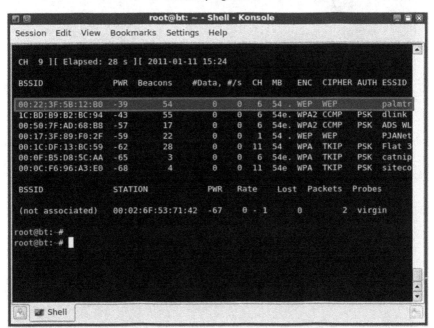

I was presented with a list of available Wireless Access Points in my area. Once I have identified the target network which was **palmtr** network, I have made notes of the BSSID (**00:22:3F:5B:12:B0**) and Channel (**6**) belonging to the Access Point

Once I have had this information, I could begin capturing packets.

To begin the packet capture, I have entered the following:

airodump-ng -c 6 --bssid 00:22:3F:5B:12:B0 --ivs -w wep mon0

I could then see the airodump program start again, but this time only showing the target Access Point.

Screenshot missing.

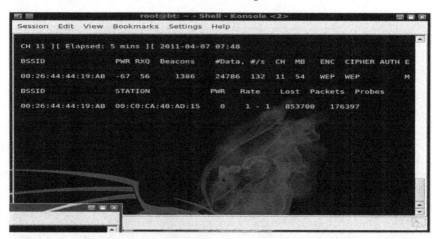

When the "Fake Authentication" was successful, I have received the following screen:

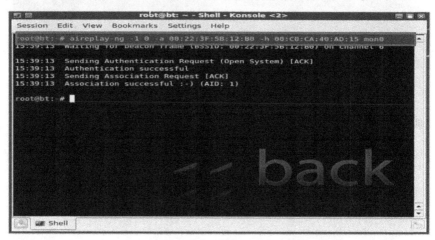

I was in the situation when there was almost no network traffic on the Access Point, It would take a significant amount of time to collect sufficient Initialisation Vectors, to allow me to crack the WEP key. However there is a method of invoking the Access Point by exchanging packets with the wireless card. This is carried out in an ARP Replay Attack. The result of this, is that a significant amount of network traffic is generated, and subsequently increases packet collection

To begin the ARP Replay Attack on the access point, the following command is entered:

**aireplay-ng -2 -p 0841 -c FF:FF:FF:FF:FF -b -h 00:22:3F:5B:12:B0 -h
00:C0:CA:40:AD: 15 mon0**

```
root@bt: ~ - Shell - Konsole <4>

Session  Edit  View  Bookmarks  Settings  Help

root@bt: ~ # aireplay-ng -2 -p 0841 -c FF:FF:FF:FF:FF -b 00:22:3F:5B:12:B0 -h 0
0:C0:CA:40:AD:15 mon0
Read 63 packets...

    Size: 234, FromDS: 1, ToDS: 0 (WEP)

        BSSID  =  00:22:3F:5B:12:B0
     Dest. MAC =  33:33:00:00:00:0C
    Source MAC =  00:24:21:F0:9D:45

    0x0000:  0842 0000 3333 0000 000c 0022 3f5b 12b0   .B..33....."?[..
    0x0010:  0024 21f0 9d45 9003 3ac6 2f00 9843 0520   .$!..E..::/..C.
    0x0020:  ee88 b0ab 39b9 3568 ad45 ed45 1387 b0aa   ....9.5h.E.E....
    0x0030:  b008 7894 8757 b8d8 bca0 5847 5d39 10bc   ..x..W....XG]9..
    0x0040:  cbc2 e27c 3c2f 30fa a425 866c f55e 0d10   ...|</0..%.l.^..
    0x0050:  6346 5949 4294 a7f5 5606 a032 9012 5d45   cFYIB...V..2..]E
    0x0060:  bb5d e3cf 3405 84c7 3d1c 49cb 455b 2245   .].4...=.I.E["E
    0x0070:  6a7e 7ebf 007b 4ddb cfca cd6a 866c 6fe9   j~~..{M...j.lo.
    0x0080:  4dda 21ba 6458 5e4e c9a2 bad8 4e0f 6c7b   M.!.dX^N....N.l{
    0x0090:  3e00 80ce 5db5 686d 80b8 8789 8158 c9ea   >...].hm.....X..
    0x00a0:  4ea8 de96 2b08 04ac a4ee 4d0d 6a1f 0689   N...+.....M.j...
    0x00b0:  4c02 1eda e785 ca19 2df7 aeea 58c3 a735   L......-...X..5
    0x00c0:  decb 45a7 c58b de72 23c1 8884 261e 2c0b   ..E....r#...&.,.
    0x00d0:  545e 7e60 12b1 787b 5ffa 0efd e05e bebc   T^~`..x{_....^..
    --- CUT ---

Use this packet ? y

Saving chosen packet in replay_src-0111-160508.cap
You should also start airodump-ng to capture replies.

Sent 5254 packets...(499 pps)
```

I have noticed the Packets per Second started to increase rapidly. According to
Tutorials typically, this will rise to between 50 - 300 Packets per second, but in my case
was around 500 packets per second.

The packet generated by Aireplay has been exchanged with the access point as can be
seen on the following screenshot. Ideally, about 50 000 has to be captured to be in with
a good chance of cracking the key.

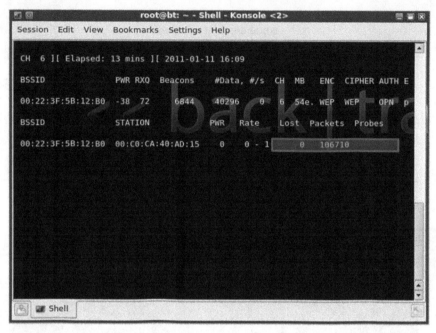

Once sufficient packets have been captured (106710), I could begin with attempt at cracking the WEP key. To crack the key, I have used the aircrack program as follows:

aircrack-ng -b 00:22:3F:5B:12:B0 wep.pak

15 seconds after I have got desired result:
> *KEY FOUND! [C9:E7:60:6A:17]*
> *Decrypted correctly: 100%*

9.3.   APPENDIX C:

CRACKING WEP PASSWORD

The goal of second experiment was to crack a WLAN secured with WEP protocol but this time I have used the access the access point of my neighbour which agreed to share his network for the time of the experiment. The only settings of the Access point I was aware of

I would have one computer (the desktop) inside the network, and my laptop trying to gain access without knowing any information about the WEP key.

In this experiment, I have used Aircrack Suite Tools to break a WEP password. Most of the commands, if not all, are in command line format. As a result, although more can be done with the command line, it is much harder to learn how to use it.

Setting Up Wireless card

Commands visible in the screenshot below starts wireless card in monitor mode.

- Airmon-ng - name of the program
- start - tells the program to start monitor mode
- wlan0 - name of network interface

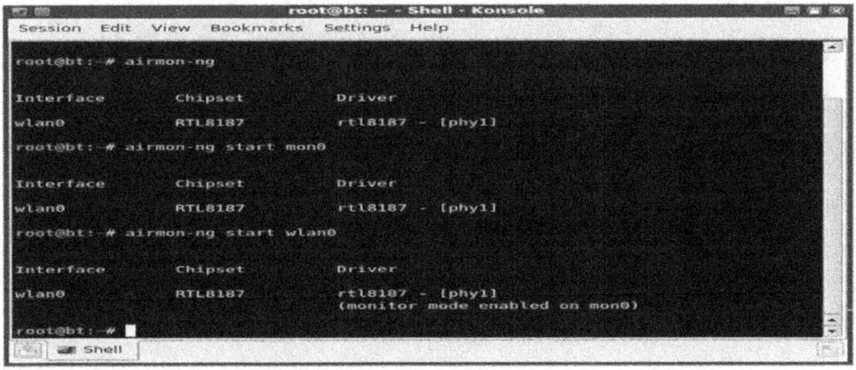

Capturing Packets

The next step is to detect nearby networks by scanning all the 14 possible channels,

The resulting window should look similar to this:

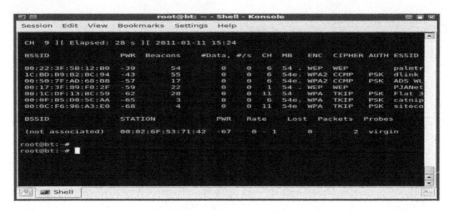

The parameters needed to perform next stage are as follows:

- BSSID

- CHENC

- ESSID

Therefore results shown on the screenshot below should be interpreted in this way: Access Point with BSSID 00:26:44:44:19:AB uses WEP encryption on channel 11, ESSID MicZ.

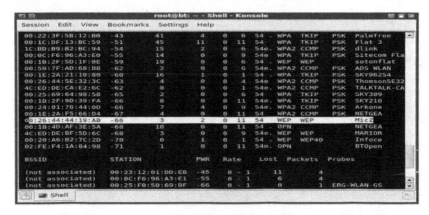

To begin the packet capture, the following command must be entered into shell console

airodump-ng -c 11 --bssid 00:26:44:44:19:AB --ivs -w wep mon0

After that the airodump program starts again, but this time only shows the target Access Point.

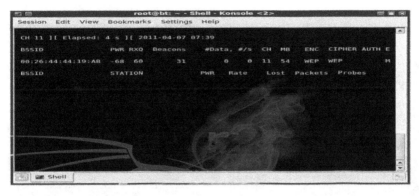

Fake Authentication

In order to be able to "inject" packets to the access point, an Associated Client must be present. That can be obtained by "Fake Authentication",

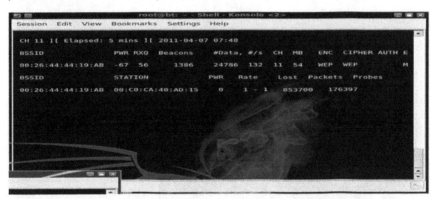

From the screenshot above can be concluded that the attacking station has been associated with the target AP.

Injecting packets

Cracking password

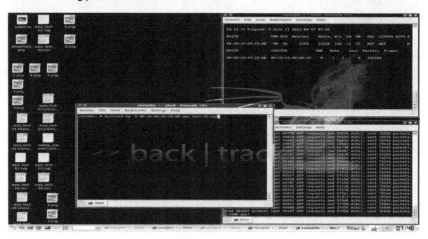

For me it took about 3 minutes to crack the key, probably because I had over a 220000 IV's (more the better).

Below is a picture of the successful password crack with use of this password to connect to the target network.

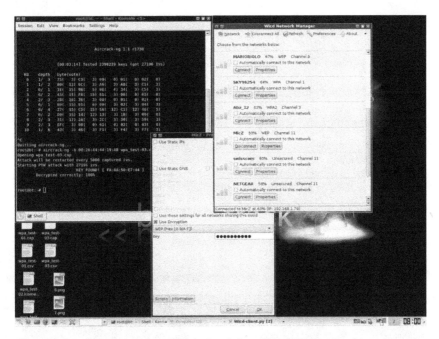

The procedure above works for a WEP protocol, for a WPA/WPA2 protocol is necessary to follow the different steps (see Appendix D).

9.4.   APPENDIX D

CRACKING WPA PASSWORD

My second goal was to crack a controlled WPA protected WLAN. Here was the same setup as the first WEP experiment, my desktop computer inside the network which knew the password (sausages) and my laptop on Backtrack Linux trying to get in.

To successfully crack WPA encryption we need to capture a full four-way handshake between a client and the Access Point. To do this we use airodump-ng just as with the WEP encryption, but this time ignoring the IVs. By capturing the 4-way handshake of WPA authentication, an offline dictionary attack can be mounted.

The detailed steps can be seen on the screenshots below

1. Setting up Wireless Card into monitor mode.

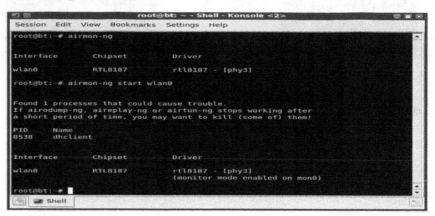

2. Capturing Packets

Airodump will capture all traffic from the ath0 network interface, including the 4-way handshake after a client has associated

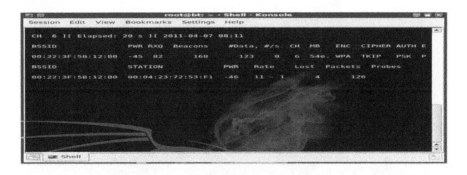

3. Capturing the Handshake

To make sure that you get a handshake, a form of packet injection can be used. In this case I have used de-authentication packets.

aireplay -0 5 -a 00:22:3F:5B:12:B0 mon0

The command above will force a 4-way handshake by transmitting de- authentication frames to everyone connected to the network. The parameter -0 5 instructs aireplay to send 5 de-authentication frames, -a 00:22:3F:5B:12:B0 sets the BSSID address of the frames to the correct address, mon0 is the WLAN interface to transmit on

Once the handshake is captured (there is one highlighted in the picture below), being near or connected to the AP is not needed as aircrack just uses the information in the packets that have captured.

I could then direct aircrack to the Wordlist. In this case, i have used password.lst with previously captured 4way handshake and has been saved in WPA_TEST-01.cap.

Aircrack have begun testing all of the words present in this wordlist. A typical keys-per-second (k/s) rate is 125 k/s. I was able to achieve an average of 170 k/s on my laptop. During further experiments on my desktop PC I was able to achieve almost 300 keys per second which have shortened the time of getting a password by a half.

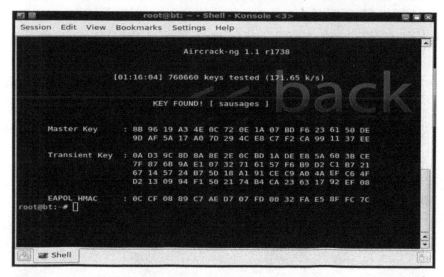

As can be seen on the screenshot above Aircrack has positively found the key. It tested 760660 keys with relatively small time of 1:16:04.

WPA may eliminate many of the problems with WEP but it is still vulnerable to attack. Cracking WPA is just simply more time consuming comparing to WEP where the cracking the key itself took only 4 seconds (see Appendix C)

9.5. APPENDIX E

WEP step by step diagram

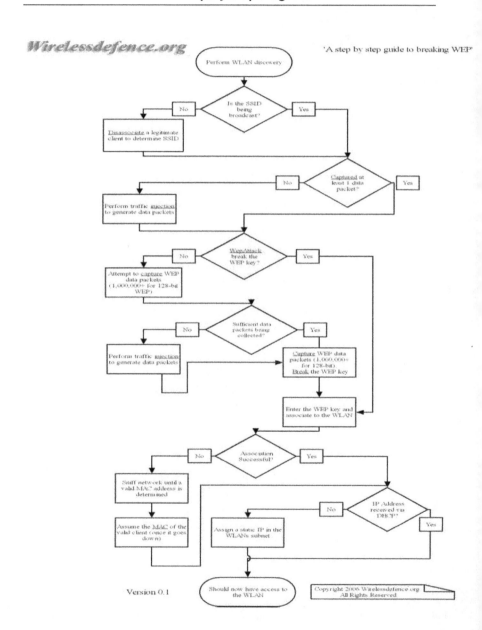

9.6.   APPENDIX F

PROJECT DEFINITION REPORT

....

....

Academic Year 2010-2011

Tomasz H

Project Definition Report

Tutor: ....

Contents

1. BACKGROUND

Wireless Local Area Networks (WLAN) are increasing within home and business uses due to the convenience, mobility, and affordable prices for wireless devices. WLAN gives mobility and flexibility to users in homes and hot spot environments, such as airports and campuses. However, WLANs have serious security problems because the wireless signal of the WLAN is broadcast through the air in all directions simultaneously. An unauthorized user can easily capture this signal using freeware tools to exploit WLAN vulnerability.

2. INTRODUCTION

The issue is not that hackers can break security measures, but that they can walk right in and take what they want. The current statistics reveal that estimated 30 percent of the market uses security appropriately; however the remaining population plugs in a wireless access point right out of the box without changing the default settings (Dowd, 2003). Moreover, users become frustrated while attempting to set up a system's wireless security features, therefore they leave it unsecured.

3. AIMS and OBJECTIVES

3.1 AIM

- To analyse aspects of wireless security in current technologies and to demonstrate the effects of the potential attacks on the network.

3.2 OBJECTIVES

- to conduct in depth research of current wireless technology availability
- to establish the operation problems in wireless medium and ways to minimize them
- to identify suitable specification for network and security appliances
- to discover unsecured wireless access points in Southampton area using *"wardrive"* technique - results and analysis
- to conduct an experiment of breaking into network secured by WEP and WPA
- to recommend possible solutions (e.g. VPN Authentication)
- to assess the effectiveness of the solution and potential risks

4. OUTLINE SPECIFICATION

This study will include experiments on the security and performance aspects in each of the alternative solutions. The security WLAN's issues will be further exposed in the practical part of the project. The various threats, vulnerabilities of WLAN will be highlighted. Furthermore, network discovery experiment will be performed and critically analysed. Problems related to confidentiality, integrity and availability of the service will be discussed. Finally, the WEP and WPA architectures, including its security status, will be further discussed based on the comparison and exposure of weaknesses of each system.

5. INFORMATION RESOURCES: LITERAURE SURVEY

The table below specifies practical resources that will be used for the research during this project. This, however, is only an outline as additional resources will be found in later development stages.

5.1	Overview of Technology and Security
BOOKS	• Arbauch, W. Edney, J. 2003, *Real 802.11 Security: Wi-Fi Protected Access and 802.11i*, Addison, Wesley. • Carter, B., 2002. *Wireless security end to end*. Indianapolis: Wiley • Chandra, P. 2008, *Wireless security*, Newnes. • Cyrus Peikari, 2006, *Maximum Wireless Security*, Sams Publishing. • Earle, A. 2006, *Wireless Security Handbook*, Auerbach Publications, Florida. • Miller, S., 2003. *WiFi security*. NY: McGraw-Hill • Sankar, S et.al. 2004, *Cisco Wireless LAN Security*, Cisco Press. • Sankar, Krishna.et. al, 2006. *Cisco wireless LAN security: expert guidance for securing your 802.11 networks*. Indianapolis, IN: Cisco
5.2	Hacking - WEP and WPA

BOOKS	• Barken, L. et.al. 2004. *Wireless Hacking: Projects for Wi-Fi Enthusiasts.* Syngress • Beaver. K. and Davis, P. 2005. *Hacking Wireless Networks for Dummies.* Wiley: Indianapolis • Cache, J., 2007. *Wireless hacking exposed: wireless security secrets and solutions.* New York: McGraw-Hill • Flickenger, R. 2003. *Wireless Hacks - 100 Industrial-Strength Tips & Tools.* Sebastopol, CA: O'Reilly • Hurley, C., 2006. *How to cheat at securing a wireless network.* Rockland, MA: Syngress • Lockhart, A., 2006. *Network security hacks. 2nd ed.* Sebastopol, CA: O'Reilly
TOUTORIALS	• WEP Cracking for Windows: http://www.brighthub.com/computing/smb-security/articles/17866.aspx • How To Crack WEP: http://www.tomsguide.com/us/how-to-crack-wep,review-451.html • WPA Cracking : http://www.speedguide.net/articles/how-to-crack-wep-and-wpa-wireless-networks-2724 • Tools Needed: http://sectools.org/crackers.html
5.3	**Hacking - Wardriving**
BOOKS	• Hurley, C et.al. 2004. *WarDriving: Drive, Detect, Defend: A Guide to Wireless Security.* Syngress : Canada • Hurley, C, et.al. 2007. *WarDriving and Wireless Penetration Testing Syngress*: Canada

6. CANDIDATE SOLUTUIONS

The main approach to be used is the comparative approach, for instance: to compare the security features and the performance characteristics of different security technologies. To compare security features of WLAN technology there would be theoretical analysis. Therefore, understanding of the concepts, architectures and practicalities of various Wireless systems and security measures will be required to ensure the experiment adequacy.

WLAN security will be thoroughly explained and demonstrated. Since WEP has the greatest number of vulnerabilities, WEP is where the main focus will be directed. WPA is interesting since it replaces WEP in many circumstances, yet it is still insecure. Therefore, the investigation and testing of WPA and WPAv2 will be documented in a comparison mode.

A number of hardware options that could be used for Project must be explored. There is such a wide range of wireless cards and antennas on the market that can be used but the trick is to select one that will be compatible to meet the project goals.

Two Intel based Acer Laptops will be used to crack the authentication key in the WEP enabled WLAN configuration. First laptop will attack the network to cause network traffic increase. Second laptop will collect (sniff) the packets required to break the encryption. It will host a program like *Aircrack* for cracking WEP key. The third party software like *Net Stumbler* may also be used to perform more precise performance testing. Additionally, WPA will be hacked using dictionary mode, where results will measure the effectiveness of the tools used during this test.

Portability between various platforms and operating systems is seen as one of the challenges. Currently, widely used tools for hacking into WEP and WPA secured networks are Linux based. If windows version could not be obtained then one of the desktop PCs would be installed with Linux operating system. It is also possible to use Virtual Machine to host Linux distributions in just one laptop.

Research report on "wardriving" and its' implications on wireless security will be proposed. In addition, different WLAN discovery applications will be tested. Finally, areas in which further research is needed to safeguard wireless networks from potential wardriving perpetrators will be addressed.

7. RISK ANALYSIS

The most common risks associated with this project are: time restrictions, resources and cost. In terms of time, the project breakdown during the first attempt can cause a delay and failure to deliver it on time. Thus, the project plan includes an additional time enabling to repeat relevant parts of the project. Advance booking will be made in case the lab room is engaged when needed.

Resource related issues may involve incompatible wireless card features resulting with an extra cost of purchasing a new card. Additionally, the drivers may unable the card to work successfully in Linux. This has a high likelihood and high potential impact due to the risk of project overrun.

To overcome this issue, testing will commence early on the most uncertain areas to ensure that they can be completed. During the network discovery experiment the antenna may not have enough gain to catch the signal, what may slow down the process or add an extra cost of purchasing a new kit. If tools acquired will not be appropriate to work with the chosen system, other solution must be investigated such as: the use of both platforms Windows and Linux. This, however links with yet another limitation, the knowledge of Linux may be insufficient leading to a delay and difficulties with the completion of the project.

Due to other assignments and exam preparation, time, which would have been spent on the Final Year Project, is lost. This could lead to missing deadlines of the project. This problem can be limited by monitoring the project more effectively and implement an additional time management system to help consider the other university work.

Additional risks associated with the project are listed in table below:

No.	Risk Area	Potential Impact	Probability of occurrence
1	Error in choosing system environment.	Critical	30%

2	Other university work pressures	Critical	50%
3	Hardware and Systems failure	Catastrophic	15%
4	Time spent on extra functionality	Minimal	20%
5	Requirement overlooked	Serious	20%
6	Error in choosing PDA device	Critical	30%
7	Project Failure at initiation stage	Serious	5%

8. REFERENCES

Dowd, T., 2003. Secure the network the same as a home: basic rules apply to keeping unwanted visitors out of prized possessions at home and at work. [online] *Communications News*, April 2003, v40 i4, p32 (1) Available: Academic One File Database

9.7.   APPENDIX G

PROJECT REVIEW REPORT

Academic Year 2010-2011

Tomasz H

Project Definition Report

Contents

Appendix A: Candidate Solutions

Appendix B: Controlled Network Plan

Appendix C: Equipment Used

Appendix D: Initial Tests Results

Appendix E: Updated Project Plan/Gantt Chart

Appendix F: Bookmarks of researched topics

1. PROJECT PROGRESS

The research phase lasted 2 weeks but was not fully completed on time because of a problem encountered within the initial testing. After identifying a substantial issue with driver configuration, the author had to conduct much further unexpected research into configuring the Linux Operating System.

Much time was spent investigating the use of VMWare to host the Backtrack Linux Distribution. The installation itself was reasonably simple; however virtual networking configuration introduced some unexpected complications. A decision was made to change the approach to live boot CD because of lack of hard drive space on the Laptop prevented a dual boot scenario.

There are problems associated with being unable to save changes or apply updates to a live boot CD.

- Wireless card drivers require firmware patching.
- The amount of Linux knowledge required was underestimated and therefore made substantial and unplanned further research necessary.

Initial experimentation phase was scheduled to last 3 weeks and was completed on time

Evidence for the above is located within the appendices and includes the following items:

- Appendix B: Packet tracer topology,
- Appendix D: Initial testing
- Appendix F: Bookmarks with research topics included

Identification of Potential Risk in Final Phase.

The impact of risk upon the completion of this project will be measurable as lost time. To compensate for unpredictable events the plan includes an allowance of an extra day every two weeks which has no specific activity. Four of these days have been allocated between the expected completion date of the final report and the submission deadline. These days are indicated on the Project Gantt by a bright green colouring.

There are several other risk factors:

Complexity

- Performing several tasks, including Packet Injection, during the practical phase may require more time than anticipated as very specific network conditions are needed.
- To compensate for this, considerable research has been performed and many technical resources have been identified.

Compatibility

- Despite significant research, a potential issue could still arise from compatibility between the chosen operating system and some of the acquired software tools. This may only become obvious at the time of use.
- To compensate, there is a variety of choice amongst Linux OS distributions. Windows based testing is also a possibility.

Equipment Failure

- The project depends upon reliable operation of a specialist wireless network card which is only available via mail order. The impact of equipment failure could result in up to a week of lost time.
- To compensate, the author has acquired another suitable but not identical wireless network card

2. OPTION ANALYSIS

After initial research, it became obvious that there is a very wide range of different technologies to investigate. The candidate solution table (Appendix A) illustrates the important factors to be considered to produce a final project specification

Research indicates that the encryption algorithms used in WEP are more suitable for this investigation as no matter how complex a chosen WEP key is; it can be easily cracked (Cache, 2010).

In contrast, WPA encryption was developed to improve upon WEP's notorious failings. It is a lot harder to crack. However, with the appropriate tools a weak WPA key can be cracked in a matter of minutes (McMillan, 2009). Initial research indicates that WPA2 may require substantially more equipment that possible for a final year project (Barken, 2004)

Initial "War Driving" type experiments provided an overview of the distribution of different types of wireless security protocols used in a sample location. As a result of this experiment, it became clear that though WPA and WEP are considered to be weaker options than the widely available WPA2, they are still widely used. (Hurley et.al, 2007).

To minimise the chances of difficulties in completing the project additional testing was performed using several Windows based software tools. However, it quickly led to the conclusion that Windows tools are very limited in capabilities. For example, unless operating in very controlled circumstances, it is nearly impossible to perform packet injection (ARP Replay Attack).

According to extensive research, particularly from Lockhart textbook and WLAN hacking related forums, an informed decision has been made to perform a penetration attack using Aircrack software suite designed for Linux. Therefore BackTrack distribution of

Linux will be used as it includes the most suitable tools to perform entire project experiments. (Lockhart , 2006)

Details of initial testing with Linux based software can be found in Appendix D.

The wireless card that I have chosen to use is Alfa AWUS036H. It is a high-powered card and features an SMA connector to facilitate the connection of an external aerial (Alfa, 2010) which is additional attribute during network discovery. It also features a Realtek 8187L chipset, which is well supported and gives very good results during vulnerability tests. (Aircrack-ng, 2010). Additional findings in chosen hardware and software has been researched and can be found in Appendix C.

To better understand the threats of wireless security including partially ineffective defence mechanisms. (Vladimirov, 2010) Thus, practical part of the project will expose the inefficiencies of some defences and then proceed to demonstrate the current best security option.

3. METHODOLOGY

According to the options analysis the most relevant methodology appears to be the following:

1) Complete research and collect resources
2) Complete randomised security assessment in chosen area (Wardriving)
3) Correctly configure testing equipment
    a. Including Operating System
    b. Including Hardware (router, laptops, wireless cards)
    c. Including Drivers and patches required
    d. Including Software
4) Start Testing
    a. Access point discovery using Netstumbler and Kismet
    b. Sniffing Traffic with airodump-ng
    c. Sniffing traffic with kismet
    d. Statistical WEP Attacks using aircrack-ng, airodump-ng, and aireplay-ng
    e. WPA-PSK dictionary attacks using aircrack-ng
5) Interpretation of results - documentation
6) Produce recommendation Report/ Guidelines
7) Write Final Project Report

4. PROJECT SPECIFICATION

The overall objective of this project is to produce a report for network managers which makes suitable recommendations for improving wireless security.

Wireless LAN networks are generally designed with emphasis on convenience rather than security. This is exactly where the problem lies. On a wireless network almost anyone with a Wi-Fi-enabled device can easily connect to and infiltrate other users systems (Misic, 2008), Therefore research based on these findings will illustrate how easy it is to protect from malicious attacks by simply using a combination of strong encryption protocol and complex key. The author will discuss the potential consequences that arise from using a weak encryption. (Cache, 2010).

The Project has two distinct phases: Research and Practical

- **Research Phase:**

This Practical Phase is limited to analysing Wireless LAN Security implementations of the weaker security protocols WEP and WPA. Despite more complex protocols being available, initial experiments and research have shown that the majority of home and small business networks still use weak wireless authentication protocols. These networks are therefore significantly vulnerable to basic online and offline attacks.

Research area will cover a wider range of encryption/authentication methods including WEP, WPA and WPA2, to provide theoretical comparison of their contrasting ability to prevent penetrating.

Several Research Questions will be investigated during the project:

- What are the problems of operating in wireless medium and how they are overcome?
- Does anybody with the laptop and wireless card can break the security of WLAN?
- What is the influence of password choice in comparison to WEP and WPA?
- What are the different types of attacks faced by wireless networks and countermeasures?
- Is the data they send through their secured wireless connection guaranteed to be confidential and maintain its integrity?

Practical Phase:

The author will attempt to demonstrate that a large number of networks still use inadequate protection by performing a data collection experiment within a randomly selected small area (2 square miles).

The next experimental phase of the project will simulate breaking WEP and WPA encryption and gaining access to a test network. A range of penetration attack strategies be described. Additionally, a detailed discussion of the steps required to perform certain complimentary attacks. This will include, for example determination of SSIDs and methods to force the access point to generate of a large number of packets. (Krishnan, 2008).Also dictionary style brute force attacks will be performed.

There are several expected outcomes hoped to be achieved as a result of using this method or approach. The research approach hopes to raise the awareness of security problems especially those related to wireless LAN security. It is hoped that reader will realise that every technology has its weaknesses and vulnerabilities, and often it is up to the users of the technology to be aware and take actions to rectify and to use these technologies consequently.

5. PROJECT PLANNING MONITORING AND CONTROL

1) Deviations from Initial Plan

After much theoretical research, the author dedicated some time to conducting practical experimentation. This enabled the author to have a better understanding of the amount of time that would likely be required to complete each stage.

Although not anticipated in the original plan it quickly became apparent that the complexity author has underestimated the level of skill required to use the Linux Operating System.

The impact of this was that additional time was required to solve issues with hardware compatibility in terms of driver availability which influenced the choice of specific OS distribution.

The author believe that this extra time was absolutely essential the progress of the project.

Only after significant experimentation did it become clear that the initial decision to use virtual machines to host the operating system would introduce unwanted complexity. As a result, the author decided to continue experimentation with a Live OS Boot CD however consideration is still being given to dedicating the entire hard disk of the host machine to Linux.

6. REFERENCES

Aircrack-ng. 2010. Compaibility Drivers. [online] Available http://www.aircrack-ng.org/doku.php?id=compatibility_drivers [accessed 10 January 2011]

Alfa Network. 2010. Product description: AWUS036H. [online]. Available: http://www.alfa.com.tw/in/front/bin/ptdetail.phtml?Part=AWUS036NH&Category=105463 [accessed 10 January 2011]

Barken, L. et.al. 2004. Wireless Hacking: Projects for Wi-Fi Enthusiasts. Syngress

Beaver. K. and Davis, P. 2005. Hacking Wireless Networks for Dummies. Wiley: Indianapolis

Cache. J and Liu. V., 2010. Hacking Exposed Wireless: Wireless Security Secrets & Solutions - - McGraw-Hill Education

Dowd, T., 2003. Secure the network the same as a home: basic rules apply to keeping unwanted visitors out of prized possessions at home and at work. [online] Communications News, April 2003, v40 i4, p32 (1) Available: Academic One File Database

Hurley, C, et.al. 2007. WarDriving and Wireless Penetration Testing Syngress: Canada

Krishnan, S. P. T., Veeravalli, B. & Wong, L. W. C. 2008. Wireless LANs (WLANs): Security and Privacy. Encyclopedia of Wireless and Mobile Communications, 1392 - 1406.

Lockhart, A., 2006. Network security hacks. 2nd ed.. Sebastopol, CA: O'Reilly

McMillan. R., 2009. Network World. "New Attack Cracks Common Wi-Fi Encryption in a Minute: Attack Works on Older WPA Systems That Use the TKIP Algorithm." [online]. Available: http://www.networkworld.com/news/2009/082709-new-attackcracks-common-wi-fi.html [accessed 5 January 2011].

Sayer. P.,2007. Don't use WEP for Wi-Fi security. Computerworld [online] Available: http://www.computerworld.com/s/article/9015559/Don_t_use_WEP_for_Wi_Fi_securit y_researchers_say [accessed 11 January 2011]

Vladimirov.A, Konstantin. V, Gavrilenko. A,.2010. Wi-Foo, The Secrets of Wireless Hacking. Addison-Wesley Buch

Misic, J.and Misic, V. 2008. Wireless Personal Area Networks : Performance, Interconnection, and Security with IEEE 802. 15. 4. Wiley-Interscience:Chichester :

APPENDIX A

CANDIDATE SOLUTIONS

	SOLUTION	Advantage	Disadvantage
OPERATING SYSTEM	Windows	Easier to operate	Fewer available tools. Traffic Injection is almost impossible using Windows.
	Linux (backtrack)	Many more software tools are available for Linux than Windows. Almost every type of attack is supported under Linux	Much more complex to operate than Windows.
	VMWare or similar Virtual Machine	Support for multiple simultaneous operating systems.	Introduces complex networking issues. Requires significant system resources and therefore affects overall performance of workstation
	Live CD	Loads straight into RAM, therefore it is possible to experiment without making changes to existing OS installation	Unable to apply essential updates. Unable to save progress to disk
	Dual Boot	Much faster, can load essential updates and save progress	Requires approximately 20GB of HDD, Potentially more complex to install.
HARDWARE	Wireless Chipset	Specific chipsets are better suited to perform penetration testing	Complex driver configuration is required
	Orinnoco Gold	Substantial documentation and drivers available	Earlier generation of wireless chipset, therefore lacks certain features such as 802.11g/n support
	Hermes		
	Atheros	More recent technology therefore enhanced features such as 802.11g/n.	Drivers are more complex to configure (patching and third party software is required)
	Realtek		
SOFTWARE	Aircrack	Simultaneous sniffing and injection of frames. Therefore reduced hardware needed. High availability of third party drivers.	Available for Windows but special .DLL file must be created to patch the drivers (complex)
	Kismet	Similar to Aircrack Suite. Kismet will work with any wireless card which supports penetration mode	Additional drivers must be patched.
	NetStumbler	works primarily with Hermes chipset, Specially used to identify network characteristics like the MAC address and Service Set Identifier (SSID) of the Access Point (AP) which are needed for further attacking purposes	the use of this tools in not characterized as a real attack

APPENDIX B

PLAN OF CONTROLLED NETWORK ENVIRONEMENT

The diagram below specifies proposed network that will be used to perform practical experiments during this project. This, however, is only an outline as additional resources will be found in later development stages.

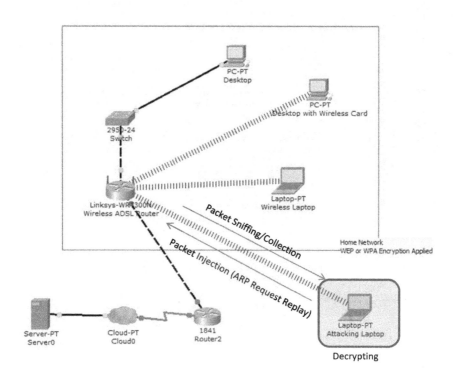

APPENDIX E : GANTT CHART

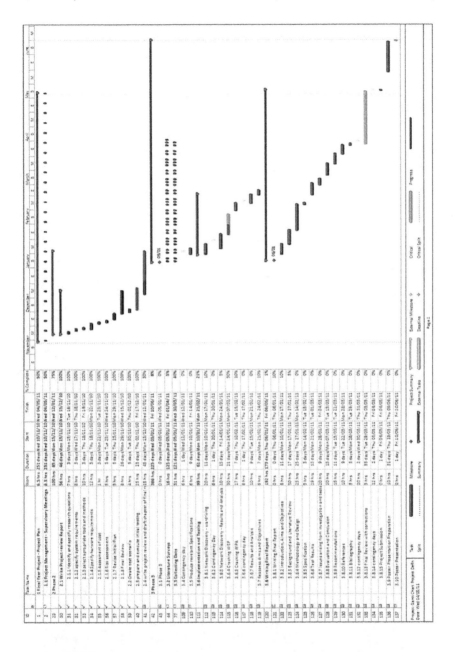

APPENDIX F

Bookmarks: Resources

Final year project toolkit - The IET	http://www.theiet.org/students/resources/final-year-project/index.cfm
Wireless security ; - Defending Wi-Fi clients	http://searchnetworking.techtarget.com/tip/0,289483,sid7_gci1259957_tax355847,00.html
CAIDA : research : security	http://www.caida.org/research/security/
Document your Network	http://it.toolbox.com/wiki/index.php/Document_your_Network#Network_Infrastructure
Wep Hack – How to Crack WEP	http://zeeloman.com/blog/2010/04/28/wep-hack-how-to-crack-wep/
Alfa AWUS036H 500mW USB WiFi Adapter – The D.U.C.K. Project	http://wiki.robotic.com/index.php/Alfa_AWUS036H_500mW_USB_WiFi_Adapter
simple_wep_crack [Aircrack-ng]	http://www.aircrack-ng.org/doku.php?id=simple_wep_crack
Cracking WPA-PSK	http://it.toolbox.com/blogs/unwired/cracking-wpapsk-6730
Ramifications of a Cracked WPA Passphrase	http://it.toolbox.com/blogs/unwired/ramifications-of-a-cracked-wpa-passphrase-27857
What you Need : How To Crack WEP - Part 1: Setup & Network Recon	http://www.tomsguide.com/us/how-to-crack-wep,review-451-2.html
Alpha card-How to Crack a Wi-Fi Network's WEP Password with BackTrack	http://lifehacker.com/5305094/how-to-crack-a-wi-fi-networks-wep-password-with-backtrack
Alfa AWUS036H + Backtrack 4 (Need help with drivers)	http://www.backtrack-linux.org/forums/beginners-forum/36170-alfa-awus036h-backtrack-4-need-help-drivers.html
cafe cracks attacks on unsecured wireless networks pdf - free unlimited eBook search and download.	http://www.ebook4.com/ca/cafe-cracks-attacks-on-unsecured-wireless-networks-tool4.pdf
Weakness in Passphrase Choice in WPA Interface - Wi-Fi Networking News	http://wifinetnews.com/archives/2003/11/weakness_in_passphrase_choice_in_wpa_interface.html
Commercial WPA/WPA2 Cracking Software Accelerated by GPUs - Wi-Fi Networking News	http://wifinetnews.com/archives/2008/10/commercial_wpawpa2_cracking_software_accelerated_by_gpus.html
WEP WPA2 Crack	http://www.ocpoint.com/WEP-WPA2-Crack.html
WPA PSK Crackers: Loose Lips Sink Ships - www.wi-fiplanet.com	http://www.wi-fiplanet.com/tutorials/article.php/10723_3667586_2
7 Things Hackers Hope You Don't Know - www.esecurityplanet.com	http://www.esecurityplanet.com/views/article.php/3891716/7-Things-Hackers-Hope-You-Dont-Know.htm
cracking wep tutorial with backtrack 3 complete tutorial| Lifclerk	http://www.lifeclork.net/cracking-wep-tutorial-with-backtrack-3-complete-tutorial.html
Hacking Techniques in Wireless Networks	http://www.cs.wright.edu/~pmateti/InternetSecurity/Lectures/WirelessHacks/Mateti-WirelessHacks.htm
Hacking Techniques in Wireless Networks	http://www.cs.wright.edu/~pmateti/InternetSecurity/Lectures/WirelessHacks/Mateti-WirelessHacks.htm#_Toc77524692
Alfa AWUS036H Wireless Network Adapter - Reviews - Memoirs of a Multitasking Mole	http://www.multitaskingmole.com/reviews/2010/2/12/alfa-awus036h-wireless-network-adapter.html
how_to_crack_wep_via_a_wireless_client [Aircrack-ng]	http://www.aircrack-ng.org/doku.php?id=how_to_crack_wep_via_a_wireless_client
compatibility_drivers [Aircrack-ng]	http://www.aircrack-ng.org/doku.php?id=compatibility_drivers
Cracking WEP with Aircrack-ng in Backtrack 4 - Tutorials - Memoirs of a Multitasking Mole	http://www.multitaskingmole.com/tutorials/2010/2/8/cracking-wep-with-aircrack-ng-in-backtrack-4.html
interactive_packet_replay [aircrack-ng]	http://www.aircrack-ng.org/doku.php?id=interactive_packet_replay#other_examples
Crack a WEP / WPA key with Aircrack-ng suite - Tips & Tweaks	http://forums.techarena.in/tips-tweaks/1364785.htm
OPNET - Getting Started with IT Guru Academic Edition	http://ict.silt.tu.ac.th/~steven/resources/itguru.html
Networking Explained. Second Edition - Books24x7	http://bcs.books24x7.com/viewer.asp?bookid=32798&chunkid=250513862
How To Crack WEP Wireless Networks For Noobs! - Video	http://www.metacafe.com/watch/1100987/how_to_crack_wep_wireless_networks_for_noobs/
What you Need : How To Crack WEP - Part 1: Setup & Network Recon	http://www.tomshardware.co.uk/how-to-crack-wep,review-1302.html
Drivers for Wireless Network Adapters - WildPackets Network Monitoring and Analysis	http://www.tomshardware.co.uk/how-to-crack-wep,review-1302-2.html
Security Solutions - TechXact	http://www.wildpackets.com/support/downloads/drivers
CS426 Spring 2009 , Computer Security	http://www.techxact.com/security-solutions.html
Index of /~crim/courses/cs647	http://homes.cerias.purdue.edu/~crisn/courses/cs426_Spring_2009/
Cracking WEP Using Backtrack: A Beginner's Guide	http://homes.cerias.purdue.edu/~crisn/courses/cs647/
Aircrack-ng - Main documentation	http://ryanunderdown.com/linux/cracking-wep-using-backtrack.php
Linux wireless LAN support http://linux-wless.passys.nl	http://aircrack-ng.org/documentation.html
	http://linux-wless.passys.nl/query_sel.php

VI.   BIBLIOGRAPHY

Books

Barken, L, et al (2004), Wireless Hacking. Projects for Wi-Fi Enthusiasts, USA, Syngress Publishing

Beaver, K., Davis P. T. (2005) Hacking Wireless Networks For Dummies, USA, Wiley Publishing

Briere, D., Bruce W.R III and Hurley P.(2003) Wireless Home Networking For Dummies, Wibley Publishing Inc. NewYork

Ohrtman, F. and Roeder, K.(2003) Wi-Fi Handbook: Building 802.11b Wireless Networks ISBN:0071412514, McGraw-Hill

Journal Articles

Begrhel, H. and Uecker, J. (2005) 'Wi-Fi Attack Vectors', communications of the ACM, August 2005, vol. 48, no. 8, pp. 21-28

Cam-Winget, N., Housley, R., Wagner, D., and Walker, J. (2003) 'Security Flaws in 802.11

He, C. and Mitchel J. (2004) Analysis of the 802.11i 4-Way Handshake [proceedings of the ACM Workshop on Wireless Security (WiSe), Philadelphia, PA, USA, [October 2004] pp. 43-50

Geng, X., Huang, Y. and Whintson, A. B. (2002) 'DefendingWireless Infrastructure Against the Challenge of DDoS Attacks', Mobile Networks and Applications vol. 7/2002, p. 213

Housley, R. and Arbaugh, W. (2003) 'Security Problems in 802.11-based networks' communications of the ACM, May 2003, vol. 46, no. 5, pp. 31-34

MacMichael, J. (2005) 'Auditing Wi-Fi Protected Access (WPA) Pre-Shared Key Mode', Linux Journal, vol. 07/2005, available http://interactive.linuxjournal.com/article/8312

Zahur, Y. and Yang, T. A. (2004) 'Wireless LAN security and laboratory designs' Journal of Computing Sciences in Colleges, vol. 19, pp. 44-60, 2004

Misc

Renderman, render (AT) renderlab (DOT) net, Stumbler Code of Ethics v0.2, http://www.renderlab.net/projects/wardrive/ethics.html Internet source produced by Renderman in Canada [accessed 20 November 2010]

Sutton, Michal (2002), Hacking the invisible network - Insecurities in 802.11x, http://www.net-security.org/dl/articles/Wireless.pdf, White paper produced by Sutton Michael, IDefense Labs, USA [accessed 20 November 2010]

Wildpacket Inc. (2003), Wildpackets' Guide to Wireless Analysis, whitepaper, http://www.wildpackets.com/elements/whitepapers/Wireless_LAN_Analysis.pdf White paper [accessed 20 November 2010]

www.ingramcontent.com/pod-product-compliance
Lightning Source LLC
La Vergne TN
LVHW092344060326
832902LV00008B/792